CONTENTS

A WALK IN CONNECTION

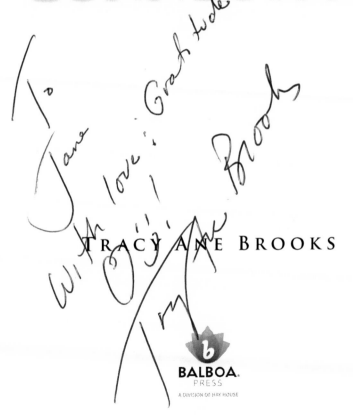

To Jane: Gratitude With love; Tracy Ane Brooks

TRACY ANE BROOKS

BALBOA PRESS

A DIVISION OF HAY HOUSE

Balboa Press books may be ordered through booksellers or by contacting:
Balboa Press
A Division of Hay House
1663 Liberty Drive
Bloomington, IN 47403
www.balboapress.com
1 (877) 407-4847

Because of the dynamic nature of the Internet, any web addresses or
links contained in this book may have changed since publication and
may no longer be valid. The views expressed in this work are solely those
of the author and do not necessarily reflect the views of the publisher,
and the publisher hereby disclaims any responsibility for them.

The author of this book does not dispense medical advice or prescribe the use
of any technique as a form of treatment for physical, emotional, or medical
problems without the advice of a physician, either directly or indirectly. The
intent of the author is only to offer information of a general nature to help
you in your quest for emotional and spiritual well-being. In the event you use
any of the information in this book for yourself, which is your constitutional
right, the author and the publisher assume no responsibility for your actions.

Printed in the United States of America.

ISBN: 978-1-4525-9832-1 (sc)
ISBN: 978-1-4525-9834-5 (hc)
ISBN: 978-1-4525-9833-8 (e)

Library of Congress Control Number: 2014919499

Balboa Press rev. date: 12/16/2014

ACKNOWLEDGMENTS

It is the creator, our planet, nature, and animals I feel most grateful for and blessed by.

To Kent Weber, my original wolf teacher, supportive partner, and inspiration. To my mom Betty, my amazing son Tamas, my wonderful brother Scott. To my dear cousin Debbie Meyers, who used her expertise of writing and valuable time to help me organize my thoughts and write A Walk in Connection. To Jenny Wagner and Snail Bob, for helping me clarify the stories and bring out the most important parts.

To the amazing photographers who generously shared their images, I am so grateful! Their images really completed the book: Gary and Lillian Crandall and Gray Crane Studios, Shevaun Williams, Terrance Heckart, Rachel Odom and Brandi Rene, Jan Frye Pinner, and Jeanne Filler Scott.

To the many people I am so grateful for and who inspire me: Jane Cane, David Nora and Peggy Kavookjian, Dr. Lenny Kloepper and River, Linda and Paul Schutt, Dave, Julie and Bruce Kreutzer, Sarah, Lauren, Madeleine and Randy Woods, Sara and Michael Stenson, Tracey Silberman Swartz and Jeffrey, Pamela Brown, Laura Jean and Vinny Passantino, Joey Chase, Lisa Benjamin and family, Luke George, Lauren Purcell, Matthew von Hobe, Gin Huffman, Irene LaRusso and her family especially Scott LaMorte, and big hugs to Alice Victor. To Betty, Ruth and Jessica Stanley, Kevin Cyr,

Ted Hubbard, Nelson Brooke and family, Thomas Bahr, Jessica McCrea, Annie White, Hilary Hastings, Ella and Duncan Graham Rowe, Leigh Vaule Steele, Kathy Bennett, Matt and Tara Ash, Stan Stiffler, Amy Sidderley, Jeff Wagner, Alan Korth, Mike Lydon, Alex Liethen, Aaron Young, Danika Oriol-Morway, Travis Moonschein, Paul Ross, Moses Cooper, Mike Gaarde, Courtney Hoyt, Jason Stewart, Rachel Milburn, Aster Wijsman, Jenny Carter and a very special thank you to Katie Torrey, Beth and Dr. Reverend Lawrence, and Kathy, Steve and Melissa of Al Zarka Arabians.

To Dr. Douglas Smith, Dr. Daniel Stahler, Rick McIntyre, Linda Thurston, Nathan Varley and Shaney Evans: I did not write about my experiences watching the wild wolves in Yellowstone National Park but the amazing opportunity to learn about wild wolves had an impact on me that helped to formulate my understanding of wolf behavior and other wild animal behavior.

I am especially grateful for Sally, who showed me that intuitive mirroring naturally occurs within each of us. To the many amazing beings who contributed but are not listed here, my hat goes off to you, thank you from the bottom of my heart! Bless each and every one of you!

To the animals that touched my life, living and past: my wolf friends Shaman, Lakoda, Cyndar, Hota, Lucus, Raven, Jordan, Zephyr, Noya, Mera, Ballazar, Dancing Bear, Ghost, Rowdy, Nikkolah, Luna, Crimzon, Navarre, Hopi, Peaches, Sabretooth, Passion, Sila, Jazmine, Hina, Bowdi, Fenris, Rami, Rasta, Asha, Nyati, Obie, Aspen, Whisper, Kestrel, Mowgali, Druid, Merlin, Beorn, Porini, Skinny, Guinness, Keechee, Sasha, Neddy, Tierra, Lily, Gizmo, Polar Bear, Magpie, Raven 2, Luna 2, Abraham, Soleil, Orion, Illiamna, Arrow, Aria, Zephir, Hailey, Max, Selway, Katimik, Nacona, Minigan, Rosie, and Tiger. My equine friends: Boo Boo, Shadow, Moses, Ikus, Red Raven, Lady Bird, Willow-Ginger, Cisco, Passion, Tammen, Majiik, Dancer, Batal, Merlin, Grinder, Brayson, Butters, and Black Jack.

Many of the experiences, understandings, and much of this text have come to me from what I believe to be divine guidance. I humbly acknowledge the tremendous support I have received from this guidance on all levels during the creation of this whole message. My deepest wish is that the words are written as intended, read with an open mind, and received with love. Lastly, I would like to acknowledge myself, for having the courage to share my story.

IIn loving memory of several very special people: Gail Holbrook Carpenter, Keith Brooks, Ruth Meyers, Kevin Honness, Lynn Donaldson and Kodi, Dr. Elizabeth Lawrence, Susan and Art Bachrach.

Seasons of the Wolf pencil sketch of Nikkolah
by Tracy Ane Brooks 1991

PART 1

Seasons of the Wolf

CHAPTER 1

Wolves in My Path

Perhaps this meeting was destiny for me, a gentle nudge to awaken me to a new level of awareness and understanding wolves.

When I was growing up, my father spent many waking hours outside alone, hidden in his garage. This was a place that he converted into a silversmith, lapidary, rock gem-cutting workshop. Inside, wooden jeweler's benches lined the walls; each one had a smooth top of Masonite wood framed in simple, raw 2-by-4 boards that finished the benches in a basic, rustic way. He had a wide variety of tools in his shop, but it was the big steel anvil that stood out like a sore thumb. He used the anvil to hammer out bracelets of sterling silver. The giant hunk of steel was painted a yellow-orange color; bolted to a large wooden stump, it was so heavy I could barely move it. The anvil sat next to an intricately designed, cast iron, antique wood stove. My father kept the stove burning in the winter, and the room stayed warm enough to work in the cold mountain atmosphere.

The cement floor seemed damp most of the time, and the moisture enhanced the petroleum smell of motor oil and gas. Combined with the unique smell of polishing compound that remained un-cleaned from the jewelry buffer, it was a very aromatic experience. My father had a unique way of creating sterling silver jewelry and unusual pieces like pickle forks and small boxes. Many of his pieces included gemstones like turquoise and jade that he himself cut and polished by hand. I can remember how much his jewelry designs resembled those of a Native American jeweler. My father always insisted he was just a silversmith as a hobby; he was not in it as a profession. He called his jewelry hand wrought. For special occasions, my mother and I would receive different earrings, rings, or bracelets.

My father prided himself on the ability to work for weeks on specific pieces, and when they were finished, he enjoyed giving them away as gifts. I was more interested in being an athlete during that time, and my favorite sport to train for was long distance running. I dreamed of one day running a marathon and trained on my own for many years. My personal best was eighteen miles at eight minutes a mile, and after training hard, running hundreds of miles, my knees began to cause me problems.

When I was in my twenties, my father taught me how to make hand wrought jewelry, and it was not long before I began to flourish, cutting out and sculpting jewelry pieces of my own design. In 1987, I started my first home business as a silversmith. I created many different earrings, pendants, pins, and more using designs I sketched up of animals, birds, feathers, and even wolf tracks. I named my new jewelry business Black Wolf Silver, inspired by a beautiful photo of a black wolf I'd found in a magazine.

I felt a strange attraction to wolves but was not sure where that feeling was coming from, as I had never been around wolves and knew very little about them. I grew up in the mountains of Colorado, with large Alaskan malamute dogs as pets; maybe that is where my affinity came from. I often took for granted the connection I felt to nature during my childhood; ever since I could walk, the mountains and forests came right up to my doorstep. During my playtime, I would roam freely with my dogs throughout the vast wilderness, oblivious and with no fear or little acknowledgment of the wild animals surrounding my home.

After working for over a year creating many jewelry pieces, I gathered my work into a collection and presented it at a small gallery opening on the Pearl Street Mall in Boulder. I immediately earned a spot as one of the featured artists and for several months ventured to sell my work there. As the months went by with minimal sales, I begin to become discouraged. I questioned my choices and longed to do more with my work than just selling at a store in Boulder. I constantly looked for opportunities that I felt would help to expand my work and be satisfying at the same time. I often donated pieces to local charities and good causes, and I entertained thoughts of someday wanting to help animals.

One day, as I sat contemplating the next jewelry design at my workbench, my father walked in the door behind me and dropped the *Daily Camera,* our local newspaper, down in front of my face. The paper landed on the desk with a photo of a striking black and silver wolf face up, staring out at me. Curious, I picked up the paper to read the article, about a place in southern Colorado called Mission: Wolf, a captive wolf sanctuary being built by Kent Weber and friends. It was 1989, and the article announced that Kent would be presenting Shaman, a black-colored gray wolf, at the University of Colorado as part of an educational outreach program, teaching people about the true nature of wolves and their importance in wild ecosystems. I decided to drive to Boulder and attend the program.

It was late March when the day arrived for the wolf program. The weather had been snowy and cold, and I was a little worried about driving my car down an icy, snow-packed mountain road. The program started in the afternoon, and thankfully, the day turned out sunny and clear. By the time I got into my car to go, the road was dry. Relieved, I eagerly drove my 1972 Chevy Malibu, fondly nicknamed "the green bomber," into the town of Boulder. While driving, I realized I had never seen a wolf up close before, except the Arctic wolves at the Denver Zoo. It felt as if I was on a bit of a mystery adventure. I had no idea what I had hoped to gain that day from my experience meeting Shaman.

Perhaps some kind of artistic perspective, something new and fresh, would creep into my consciousness. Besides, bettering my understanding of this legendary creature could do nothing but enhance my mind and my arts on all levels. And as a contribution to the wolf sanctuary, I created wolf-themed jewelry pieces to give as a donation. My hope was the jewelry would be sold as a fundraiser for Mission: Wolf and the money used to help with a project such as fence construction. Before I left the house, I tucked a small box packed with earrings, pendants, and pins inside my pants pocket. I was growing excited to see Shaman the wolf and hopeful for an opportunity to meet Kent in person.

I arrived a half an hour early at the university. Right away, I found a parking place large enough to park the big car. The lot was located across the street from several large stone buildings where I thought the program was being held. I was determined to find the right building quickly but anxiety came up in my stomach when I walked into the first building. I paused and realized I was standing in the wrong place. Discouraged I hastened my pace and found the building across the street was where I needed to be.

When I was in the second grade, in addition to repeating the grade again, I was required to attend summer school due to my inability to focus and pay attention to school work. My summer school classes were held at this very same campus. At that young age, I felt especially embarrassed and insecure about many things. And those feelings were now rushing back as I looked around the familiar architecture inside the building. I felt like a fish out of water and quickly sat at the first desk I could find. As I waited I remembered why I was in the room in the first place, I smiled and wondered what it was going to be like when the wolf entered the room? I asked myself, momentarily distracted from the awkward out of place feeling in the pit of my stomach.

I was growing more excited as the moments ticked by, and then, very humbly, Kent walked in to the room. I recognized him immediately from the photo in the newspaper article, but he was much more striking in person than on newsprint. After a brief introduction by one of the students, Kent began to speak. I liked the sound of his voice; there was something about it, I could not pinpoint exactly what that something was. It just resonated in my mind. Kent was a tall, slender man with a handsome face and intense blue eyes that flashed as he looked around the room; he seemed at ease in front of the audience. He appeared confident as he spoke about his experiences living with wolves and why he was inspired to travel with a wolf to school.

"Shaman was born in captivity," he said, "and can never be returned to the wild."

Even though Shaman was not wild, nor had he ever been a wild or free-roaming wolf, he had the instincts and behaviors of a wild wolf, except one important aspect: Shaman was brave enough to walk in front of groups of people, appearing in public as a teacher.

Kent explained, "Shaman did not live like a pet inside the house."

Shaman was very different from a dog; the wolf would grow up to become an independent, wild-minded animal. Kent talked about how he understood that while Shaman was young and docile, he was somewhat manageable. As an adolescent, Shaman was dependent on Kent for his basic survival needs like food, water, vet care, family structure, socialization, affection, play, and even dominance.

Shaman's instincts were not the same as an obedient domesticated dog. They were similar in many ways, but intensified, more amplified, backed by the raw power of wild nature. Dogs remain in a state of puppy-like attitude and personality through out their lifetime, while wolves mature to different levels of independence. Kent gave the audience a short insight into why he and Shaman traveled to schools and presented educational programs about wolves. And after a brief explanation of how the wolves greeted each other, Kent finished with a request to please stay quiet and seated when he left the room and remain so, especially when he returned with Shaman.

Kent disappeared out the classroom door, leaving behind the crowd of students surrounding me, all sitting still. To my surprise, I heard only a few, slight whisperings here and there. The entire room was quiet and still. Then Kent returned to the door. A sound wave of reaction filled the room: "Ahhh!" Numerous voices expressed their awe toward the large black wolf entering the room.

I was surprised at the size of Shaman. He was much larger than I thought he would be; in so many ways, Shaman was different than any dog I had ever seen. In that instant, all the preconceived notions I had of how Shaman would look or act disappeared. He was nothing like what I thought he'd be. It was hard to believe that Shaman was only ten months old. His head seemed somewhat out of proportion to the rest of his ninety-pound body. He stood scanning the room under his oversized, jet-black ears, up on his very long, stilt-like legs. I could see how big his feet were from clear across the room; they were huge.

Shaman and Kent stayed centered in the front of the room, and I could not help but stare at the gangly awkwardness of the adolescent wolf. Almost a year old, his appearance was obviously a growing phase. He looked nothing like the beautiful, thick-furred wolf from the photos in the magazine. Still, I could not take my eyes off of Shaman as he moved; I imagined he possessed abilities and moves that I would probably never see or even fathom. Kent was not bad to look at either, but I knew he was married, so I did not give it another thought. I focused on how Shaman carried himself and visualized the stunning potential the young wolf would grow into. Shaman moved around Kent's legs, pausing at different times to survey his surroundings, taking in every move or noise within his immediate vicinity. I watched the wolf drop his head down and press his nose into the tiled floor.

The wolf became curious and began to sniff. Kent must have realized how difficult it was for those of us who were sitting up in the back rows to see Shaman. He started to move Shaman toward the stairs. Shaman kept his eyes up and head down as he walked, sniffing and watching the people in the front. They intently watched Shaman right back. Kent explained how he had seen tragic consequences when pet wolves did not work out in domestic home situations. In many cases, the animal was not to blame for problems arising in the relationships between the wolf and human.

"Wolves rarely make good pets," he said, "and because of this, Mission: Wolf is often requested to take in unwanted pet wolves and wolf dogs, more than the sanctuary could physically house."

Kent stated that most of the wolves living in pet situations often did not make it over three years old.

"At Mission: Wolf," he added, "Shaman lives outside in a large natural enclosure, mimicking a small wild habitat. And although still under construction, his habitat contains other canines like him for companionship."

Kent followed Shaman around the room, letting out a little slack on his leash. It appeared to me that Shaman was leading Kent on a journey, driven by his wolf nose. For a brief moment, Shaman went out of sight, blocked by all the eager people in front of me, who were just as excited to see him as I was. I could see Shaman peek around the corner, sniffing the shoes of a few students. Randomly, a shoe from a person or the leg of a desk would attract the wolf's attention.

Shaman appeared more interested in smelling and less interested in engaging with the audience. After a few seconds of investigation, he moved his nose under the chairs and beyond the desk legs. He seemed tame and surprisingly domesticated, walking around a room full of people. Nearly every student in that drab, slightly stale-smelling classroom sat quietly fixed on that black wolf, the brightest light in the room. I don't know if the other people were paying attention to Kent's presentation or not. All I remember was that I missed what was being said every time Shaman came into view. His dark fur was overgrown, broken off in places, and matted up against his hips and shoulders.

His coat seemed unusual, tufts of fur like dyed cotton ball clouds appeared to float at his sides. The wolf photos I had previously seen showed animals in their thick winter coats, ready to survive the harshest of freezing environments. I was intrigued and wanted to see the texture of Shaman's fur up close; it looked so rich and inviting.

As I watched him sniff around, I thought of a German shepherd's profile; it was comparable to the wolf's big head.

Shaman's large ears stood straight up on his head, like satellite dishes that rotated independently (they seemed to search for the most interesting sound). I thought he could hear a lot better than I could, based on the size of his ears. As Shaman began to walk up the stairs, I really noticed that his walk was much different from any dog I had seen. In a quick burst of movement, he bounced up a few stairs at a time, with similar fluidity as a gaited horse would display, or even a cat. In comparison, my dogs would have bounced or waddled up the stairs.

Wolves are agile creatures that can travel long distances gracefully, without tiring or wasting important energy by keeping their pace at an easy jog. What helps wolves conserve energy, when they run in a straight line, their tracks create what is called a "registered track," which means that as the wolf trots, the rear foot hits the same spot the front foot landed. In snow or mud, wolf tracks can appear as if there is only one set of two tracks. Upon closer examination of the tracks, often eight toenails usually can be counted in one paw print. Sometimes the outline where the smaller rear foot has overstepped the front track can be seen too. The way Shaman carried his big front feet only exaggerated his cat-like walk.

Shaman's hips glided in a graceful, even, and collected way. Overall, he seemed relaxed, moving in long smooth strides; his back was built like a table, flat and rectangular. Kent asked everyone to stay seated while he walked Shaman up the stairs toward the back of the room. As they moved toward where I was sitting, I caught the first glimpse of the amazing coloring on Shaman. Mixed throughout his rich jet coloring, warm, inviting reddish brown and mahogany tones, blended with white, silver, and black. *What a beautiful combination,* I thought to myself. I loved these colors in his fur and thought how very unique they looked. I had no idea that black wolves had that much depth of color in their coats.

His face was intense and striking; now that he was getting really close, I could see him better. Silver streaks marked his chin, shoulders, belly, and hips. A large white star on his chest appeared as he took another step up, facing in my direction. Shaman's slinky, long black legs tapered inward like a designer dress, exaggerating his hip movement. I could hear his toenails tap the white cement floor as he came up the stairs. As Shaman came closer to the back of the room where I was, Kent repeated his request for the audience to stay put in their seats. He explained that Shaman would become nervous around men, and if anyone stood up or walked toward him, his first instinct would be to get away as fast as possible.

That meant the wolf and Kent would disappear out the door and end the wolf program. As I studied Shaman, he seemed to be a very sensitive creature. I noticed his mannerisms, the delicate way he was checking everything out, using his nose and then his eyes. I know his hearing was playing a role as well, even though it was not visually obvious. I looked around behind me and saw everyone still watched him as intently as I was. A wave of quiet anticipation went through my gut as I turned my focus back to Shaman.

It was wonderful how quiet and respectful everyone was; Kent talked about how shy wolves really were, and the audience seemed to really understand. Shaman, on the other hand, was not paying much attention to the words coming out of Kent's mouth. The wolf appeared completely uninterested and in his own world. Still heading in my direction, Kent and Shaman were slowly weaving their way through the rows of students. I completely blocked out what Kent was saying; as Shaman came back into my view, I became fixated on the wolf. When Shaman went out of sight behind the row of desks, I caught what Kent was saying. Now that Shaman was almost right in front of me, I was mesmerized, feeling as if this was some kind of daydream.

As Shaman walked down the row of seats directly in front of me, I could see the top of his fur, over the desks, in between the people. Long black guard hairs ran down the back of his neck and gave him a lion-like mane. This mane really emphasized the matted and scruffy broken fur that adorned his shoulders, hips, and sides. I vaguely remember hearing Kent tell everyone to look closely at his eyes. Kent encouraged everyone to take the opportunity to see the amazing eyes of the wolf up close as Shaman passed. Shaman had grown accustomed to people looking at him, but Kent warned never to look wild animals or even unfamiliar dogs in the eye for any reason. Even domestic dogs can become threatened and aggressive if a person looks directly into their eyes.

Shaman walked closer to my seat, and when he did, the hair on my arm stood up. I barely remember Kent finishing the eye-to-eye contact part, when Shaman's face came into my full view. I first saw how narrow his nose was as he lifted his head off the floor to sniff the edge of my chair, where my knee was. I was not quite prepared for the impact of this brief yet powerful encounter; the wolf's eyes and my eyes locked for an instant. I paused as an unnerving feeling washed through me. I felt vulnerable but in a different way than I had ever experienced before. A cold sensation went up my spine and caught me off-guard. The only way I can explain the effect of being within a few feet of Shaman's face and eyes (beyond the physical appearance of his bright yellow eyes that flashed a lime green, worm shaped squiggle in the corner) was the intense energy radiating from them.

Shaman's eyes were so vivid and full of energy. Pure and good energy, not evil, villainous energy like that of a horror film. Perhaps this meeting was destiny for me, a gentle nudge to awaken me to a new level of awareness about wolves. For some people, it was a challenge to see the wolf as a divine creature with a purpose. To me, the wolf held a sacred place in the wilderness and deserved respect and gratitude. A flood of emotions came over me as the brief contact ended. As quickly as Shaman appeared in front of me, he disappeared and was gone.

A faint smell of cedar lingered as Shaman moved on to the next row of eager souls, awaiting their chance to see the incredible wolf up close. What an encounter. Burned into my mind's eye was that brief and intense eye-to-eye moment with Shaman. I later learned that due to the power of eye contact, alpha wolves frequently tend to divert looking directly into other pack mate's eyes. It may be a way to avoid potential conflict.

"Shaman is different," Kent said. "He is being raised with the goal that he would stay comfortable when people look into his eyes."

The ability to see the wolf eye to eye was a great educational tool. If every human had the opportunity, like I did that day, to look into a wolf's eyes (the windows of the wolf's soul), perhaps their perception of wild wolves would be different, the relationships with our wild animals more intuitive and connected. For sure, I felt that there was far more to the wolf than we as humans understood, and had yet to discover. I believed it was well worth taking the time to learn and explore as much as possible about this amazing creature.

As I pondered what had just happened, I sat there thinking about the difference between the eye to eye encounter in comparison to any dog I had known. I had never been struck emotionally in the way I had meeting Shaman that day. It was true for me the color of Shaman's eyes were different from a dog's eyes. My dogs had deep brown eyes. But in the low light of the dimly lit classroom, Shaman's eyes reflected the color of a golden aspen leaf, flashing in the fall sunshine. But as beautiful as his eyes were, it was not the color that captured me. It was the deep, pure essence of Shaman that inspired me, the light beaming through the color that I connected with.

I did not understand what any of my feelings meant that day, nor could I put them into words that had any meanings. I could not remember any more of what Kent was saying, either. I was back to daydreaming. I found Shaman fascinating, and if the eyes were the windows to the soul, wolves had something to teach me. There were no books that I could find written about this deeper emotional side of the wolf, only introductions to it. To me, Shaman's eyes held a deeply engrained wisdom, a powerful presence and confidence that felt natural, instinctual, with ancient connections to the earth.

On one hand, I felt scanned by this animal, like I could not hide anything from Shaman. On the other hand, I felt like I had just been handed an incredible gift. How honored I was to have had a brief stare with a wolf. I knew I wanted to travel and see Mission: Wolf, the place where Shaman lived. After the program ended, Kent walked Shaman back outside and then returned and talked with many of the students. I waited around, looking for an opportunity to talk with Kent. I remembered watching as he stood at the top of the stairs. He was surrounded by dozens of interested college students and me, all wanting to learn more about what they could do to help wolves, Mission: Wolf, or some other cause.

When it was my turn, I too expressed an interest in helping Mission: Wolf; specifically, I wanted to donate jewelry to be used as a fundraiser. I pulled the small box of jewelry out of my pocket and handed it to Kent; he opened the box, looked up at me, and smiled. I left the university that day, inspired to make more jewelry for Shaman's sanctuary. I could not wait to get back to work at my jewelry bench. I also told Kent that if he ever needed help with the traveling education program, or with the animals themselves, to give me a call. I had no idea how or what I could do to help. I just knew I sincerely wanted to help. And for the next month, I spent every day at my workstation, making as many different wolf track jewelry pieces as I could, all the while planning my visit to Shaman's home.

CHAPTER 2

Wolf Sanctuary

If eyes act as windows into the soul, looking into Cyndar's eyes would mark the beginning of my life with wolves.

On a warm spring day in 1989, I arrived at Mission: Wolf for the very first time. After a four-hour drive from Boulder, I had anticipated dropping off a tray of jewelry pieces I had recently created. I drove the green bomber up a steep dirt driveway that led into the sanctuary. I parked my car and got out. Stretched and looked around the sanctuary; it was more beautiful and remote than I originally thought. The air was cold and crisp, and the smell of spring blooming was everywhere. They had found a great scenic spot to build a wolf sanctuary. Surrounded by a tremendous panoramic view of the Sangre De Cristo Mountain range, it was impressive.

To my surprise, a tall, vibrant young man immediately greeted me with a welcoming smile on his face. He explained to me that Kent and Shaman had left on a trip to Santa Fe, New Mexico, visiting school kids, the previous day and were not expected back for a few days. I could not help but feel a surge of disappointment; I believed Kent knew I was coming. But I quickly forgot about it as the young man gave me a tour of the facility. I especially became intrigued when I saw in the distance a large enclosure with several wolves standing at the fence, looking over at us.

I was awestruck; the wolf sanctuary was a new and evolving non-profit organization, short on money for building fences and general operating expenses, yet it was perfect for wolves. Kent and his friends wanted to build a place where the wolves could live as if they were wild, where people could observe the wolves, learn from them, perhaps even become inspired by them. Most importantly, the wolves had enough space; they could be far enough away from people if they chose.

Occasionally, chain link fence was outright donated; that made a huge impact on the overall size of the enclosures. At the time, the size of the wolf habitats were like no other zoo I had ever seen. They were securely constructed from eight-foot heavy gauge chain link; an additional section of four-foot ground mesh was sewn to the bottom, partially buried into the ground. Dead trees were stripped clean of sharp branches and rolled out flat over the ground mesh and wired to the edge. This helped hold the wire down flat and kept the wolves from crawling underneath the mesh. The ground mesh was then filled over with rocks and dirt, buried to help prevent injuries to toes and feet. The same type of wire mesh fencing was sewn on top as an overhang, bringing the total height of the enclosures up to twelve feet tall (even more in some places).

But it was not the steel fence that made the enclosures amazing; it was the element of wild that struck me. Inside the spacious, natural habitats, tall ponderosa pines loomed over land filled with lots of aspen trees and other foliage, radiating a wonderful feel. It was apparent that one of the goals was to leave the place as close to how Mother Nature created it as physically possible. It was incredible to see the wolves living at this sanctuary. The wolves seemed to be vibrant, happy creatures (considering they were living in captivity). It was as if they were reflecting the feel of the atmosphere. One thing I remember noticing right off was how different and unique each and every wolf was. Their coats and markings were interesting and beautiful: thick fur resembled spiked lamb's wool, guard hair tips, sticking straight up and out.

16

I spent the night at the sanctuary, tossing my sleeping bag down on the couch in the office trailer. Surrounded by photos of the wolves, newspaper clippings tacked to the walls, and a cage that contained a couple of finches tucked up on the highest perch. The tiny birds were sleeping soundly, huddled up close to one another for the night. The wolves howled several times, waking me up. It was cold, and I was having trouble staying warm. As I lay quietly, listening to the wolf sounds in the dark, unfamiliar room, I noticed the different tones each wolf had.

After one wolf started to howl, they all howled. Once the howl was over, each wolf seemed to end at the same time and on the same note. The sound of the howling was incredible, haunting, but in an intriguing way. I loved listening to them. The wolves were more amazing than I ever imagined they would be. When the next morning arrived, I awoke refreshed to more howling. After the opportunity to meet and spend time with the wolves living at the sanctuary and experiencing all the howling of the previous night, I begin to see that each wolf was rather extraordinary in its own unique way.

Of the wolves I met face to face that day, one stood out. Her name was Cyndar. She was alpha female of her pack, which included Nikkolah, Lucus, Raven, and Jordan. Cyndar was a tall, slender, and endearing black wolf with silver and white markings similar to Shaman. She came right up to me in her enclosure. I sat down on a wooden bench and watched her approach me; it was overwhelming and wonderful. She was confident and curious as she came right up to sniff my nose and face.

I held my face still and received a few licks on the lips and nose. Cyndar made me feel completely relaxed in her home. The others in the pack came up and greeted me too, but it was Cyndar who made me feel safe. When I looked into her eyes, I was immediately catapulted back to that first meeting of Shaman and that radiant, unspoken intensity. Pools of deep, amber brown reflected Cyndar's bright inner light, shining out at me. Her eyes were a different shade than Shaman's, I remembered from that brief encounter. But they had the same "reach out and touch me" effect that I experienced with Shaman at the university.

I did not know this after just two days at the sanctuary, but those wolf eyes and howls would become more familiar than I could ever imagine. If eyes act as windows into the soul, looking into Cyndar's eyes would mark the beginning of my life with wolves.

The sanctuary offered the wolves large, spacious enclosures and a raw meat diet; they were living as if they were in a small version of the wild. But unlike wild wolves, these captives had the extra benefit of human caretakers. The enclosures were built in the middle of the wilderness. Aspen trees filled the valley. They were scattered among and under huge ponderosa pine trees that towered above the sanctuary, and the joint forest spread up the top of the ridge behind the sanctuary. The wolves really seemed to feel at home in this setting under the trees, waiting and watching as people worked to feed, water, and care for them.

I was concerned about being high up in the Rocky Mountains of Colorado and having to drive on bad roads, so I headed back home that afternoon. I took one last look around this amazing place before I loaded my bag into the green bomber, which was great fun on the highway but not built for four-wheel driving in the mountains. I missed Kent and Shaman that trip but believed I would meet up with them another time. A week later, Kent called my house to apologize for missing my visit, and then he asked if I wanted to accompany him the following week on a short trip, taking Shaman to a school in Santa Fe. I got an excited but nervous twang in my gut.

I was worried what my parents might think; I was sure they would disapprove, even though I was in my late twenties. I was certain neither of my parents had considered this as a career path for me: traveling to New Mexico to lead a wolf into school and teach about the wild canine. The trip would take a few days, meaning I would be camping with a man I had just met. This would be a huge change from living at home with my parents and making jewelry.

To my pleasant surprise, after talking briefly with my mother, she supported the idea. My father, however, was more conservative. He sometimes had a negative attitude towards the family dogs (or really any animal that walked through the door of our house).

Growing up, I remember my father frequently cursing at some animal or another. My dad usually stepped in the poop left on the floor after someone had an accident (sometimes, it seemed those incidents were no accident). Dad, I believed, would rather see me stay at my jewelry bench, working on the new family tradition of jewelry making, than pursue a volunteer job working with wild animals. Regardless he did not object to the idea of me going, that was a relief!

CHAPTER 3

Traveling with a Wolf

During the drive to New Mexico, Shaman spent the entire time sitting on the back seat, completely ignoring me.

It was April when I arrived at the wolf sanctuary for the second time. I loaded my bags into the tan and yellow 1979 Chevy van parked in the driveway. The thought of riding in that van with a huge black wolf, a large red malamute dog named Lakota, and a man I barely knew was intriguing and scary at the same time. But something inside me urged me to go for it, to take a risk. After spending a few hours preparing for the drive, talking to Kent and the others at the sanctuary, I found it easier to relax. Kent had a very gentle demeanor and showed the utmost respect toward Lakota and Shaman. My thinking was, someone who had that kind of connection with animals had to be a good person.

I also had the opportunity to spend a few minutes by myself with Lakota before we left that day. He was a sweetheart of a dog and one of Shaman's trusty, easygoing companions. I never realized it, but another companion named Hota, a wolf malamute cross, had been with Shaman the very first time I saw them at the university. I was so transfixed on Shaman, I never noticed Hota. Kent told me that Lakoda would be my responsibility during the trip. If I handled

Lakoda, Kent could give his full attention and focus on the audience and Shaman.

The traveling wolf van was customized to carry Shaman and Lakoda. The van was small, considering such a large presence as Shaman was to be contained inside. It was built with an opened space in the center and a sitting bench. Behind the bench at the back of the van was a steel mesh kennel, a secure holding pen to contain the big wolf when we needed to keep the van doors open to load or unload. The kennel door could easily be secured to stay open and allow the two canines free range of the van interior. I did not know what to expect, as it was the first time I had spent one-on-one time with a wolf in a van. During the drive to New Mexico, Shaman spent the entire time sitting on the back seat, completely ignoring me, looking out the window. He seemed to be pretending I was not even there.

I could respect that and did not want to push Shaman, so if the wolf wanted to ignore me, I decided to ignore him right back. I became focused talking to Kent and attending to Lakoda during the drive. I was fascinated to learn about Kent's experiences with wolves. Getting to know Lakoda was a blast too. He loved attention, just as you would expect a dog to, and unlike Shaman took advantage of any pets I would give out. As we traveled down the road, Lakoda sat between Kent and me.

The programs were hectic and full of energy. People were buzzing about Shaman's visit to their school. Kent shared information about the sanctuary that I had not heard yet, and I found myself learning as much as the students were. After three days of ignoring one another in the van, in the programs and on walks, Shaman finally began to take notice of me. Very minimally, mind you, but there were glimpses of curiosity. At first, he maintained a clear distance and aloofness. I would soon learn to dance on eggshells around Shaman in order to be accepted by him. This began an unfolding of many lessons to come into the intricate mind of an adolescent wolf, revealing to me a deeply instinctual creature with no desire to please anyone.

Unexpectedly, during that road trip, Kent and I hit it off romantically, in a wonderful way. The timing was good for both of us to consider being in a relationship. Kent had already split from his wife, and I was single. Quite frankly, it seemed the cards were dealing me a new fate. This too may have been part of the reason why Shaman did not immediately warm up to me. The wolf must have sensed the energy sparking between the two humans. Or perhaps it simply came down to respect in the pack hierarchy. To Shaman, Kent was his leader, the alpha, and that may have been why he was hesitant to approach me at first; regardless, I could speculate all day and still not have an answer as to why Shaman was ignoring me.

During exercise stops we made along the way, I learned something interesting about Shaman's personality. He would get scared if anyone ran up close behind him, especially if he was lost in his own thoughts and enjoying his time (that was pretty much all the time). We parked the van on a deserted dirt road, put the long leashes (reserved especially for running) on Shaman and Lakoda, got out, and started moving down the road. I jogged ahead, gaining speed, when, without thinking, I stepped out of Kent's way. Lakoda's leash was dragging on the ground, and I worked to correct it, when the next thing I knew, I was right behind Shaman, and then it was too late: I had already violated Shaman's silent rule of space.

The second Shaman became aware of my body flinging toward him, he bolted sideways and back, just enough to get out of my way. He then stopped running, turned, and faced me with his tail slightly tucked under his belly. Kent thought it might help Shaman get over his resistance toward me if I ran with (or rather next to) him. Yeah, right! I wondered how that was going to work. I loved running, and fitness was always important to me. In my teen years, I took up long-distance running and worked to keep myself in the best shape I could. I liked to think of myself as a cheetah that could run fast for short distances or slow down and pace myself for a longer haul. But that was in my daydreams.

I found Shaman's fast-paced bursts, combined with abrupt stops, difficult to keep up with and impossible to stay ahead of (especially when he veered off course to avoid me). When I thought about it, I realized that this reaction he was having made sense. I believed anyone would do the same in response to someone unfamiliar running right up behind them. I was oblivious to how I affected Shaman; I was learning, but ultimately, I was not very aware of my own body language (or my body, for that matter). One of the pitfalls of leading such an active life was the wear and tear on my body, which was full of misalignments. The years of pounding the pavement had taken its toll on my back and knees. I was trying to be graceful and carefully run around Shaman, but due to the thud of my feet landing in a disconnected way on the hard road, Shaman turned and looked at me as if to say, "What are you doing?"

I quickly learned that by handling Lakoda at Shaman's side and paying no mind to the big wolf, I could run comfortably next to Shaman without causing him to bolt. By doing this, I started to get closer to Shaman. On the return trip back to Colorado, he was a little more comfortable with me. He now watched me as I sat in the front passenger seat. I even caught him sneaking up for attention, using Lakoda as his safety. I was petting Lakoda and noticed out of the corner of my eye Shaman standing behind him, watching curiously. He did not want me to touch him yet, and I had no need to push my limits to try, but I could hardly wait to get my hands on his luxurious fur.

CHAPTER 4

Becoming Acquainted

I wanted to learn everything about wolves, to study how they lived and behaved, anything and everything. Wolves fascinated me.

Not long after that trip, Kent and I began our relationship. One day, he took me on a walk, which ended at a small wooden cabin he was building in the trees behind the wolf enclosures. He looked directly at me and said he was hoping to complete the building with someone special. That summer, I moved to the sanctuary, a place that became very romantic and special to me. I loved living in the mountains; I became a director of the sanctuary, working more and more every day with the wolves and learning to share my stories as a teacher. I did not have my jewelry worktable set up, so I spent my time focusing on the animals. I wanted to learn everything about them, to study how they lived and behaved, anything and everything. Wolves fascinated me.

Kent gave me a little information about how the wolves got their start living at the sanctuary. The refuge really gained momentum after the arrival of several homeless wolf pups. Three of the wolves had been born on a Wisconsin dairy farm. The wolf parents were being kept for breeding. The dairy farmer had a side business, selling wolves and wolf dogs to anyone interested. As the pups grew, they would drink milk directly from the teat of the cow as it was squirted into their mouths. The pups had free run of the land and were seen running loose behind the cows through the cornfields. A concerned neighbor recognized that if the pups were left loose, they would likely meet an early demise, and she helped the farmer find responsible homes for them.

Kent originally promised to give only one pup a home, but he ended up taking in three. Midsummer of 1987, three young wolves were transported from Wisconsin to their new home at the sanctuary. All three siblings were striking: black with silvery white markings. The male was called Lucus, and his two sisters named Raven and Jordan. Raven was named after the magnificent and brilliant *Corvus corax*, which frequented the trees and grounds around the sanctuary, scavenging on leftover meat scraps. Lucus, Raven, and Jordan were introduced to the other wolf pups, Nikkolah, Noya, and Zephyr, already living at the sanctuary.

Nikkolah, a curious and determined young wolf, was the oldest and largest of the pups; he exhibited leadership over the newly established puppy pack. He was prone to mischief, a sure sign of what was to come as he matured. A small part of each pen was temporarily constructed using six-inch steel mesh. The squares were small enough to keep adult wolves in, yet big enough that little wolves could squeeze their tiny bodies through and move freely around the adult canines. Ultimately, these homeless wolf pups would choose an adult and find their pack for life.

One day, the pups squeezed their way inside with Hota. Gruff Hota was a big grizzly bear-like mix with rich, dark black and brown fur. Hota's fur was so thick, it seemed the only place it could go was straight out from his body. He was not a pure wolf; he was a wolf dog cross; he was one-quarter wolf and three-quarters malamute. Not being a pure wolf did not affect how the puppies reacted to him. They used the same behavior around Hota as they did with Cyndar, a pure wolf. The pups would jump up at Hota, nipping and pulling at the big bear's mouth, begging of food.

The pups were always happy to see Hota and eagerly wagged their little tails, making sweet high-pitched noises. Hota would growl fiercely and stand tall with his tail curled up high on his back; the pups would fall down on their backs, wiggling and being submissive to him, begging for attention and acceptance. Hota was dignified, growling and grabbing their little heads and necks with his teeth, biting down with a controlled grasp, not hard enough to hurt the pups. Even with all the discipline from the adults, the babies continued to frequent the different enclosures. This phase did not last long, because their fat little bellies and big heads soon outgrew the fence squares. Still, for as long as they could cram themselves through the wire squares, they would try.

The time soon came to move them from the puppy pen to their new destination: the big wolf pen. It was the largest enclosure at the sanctuary, spanning approximately one acre in size. The plan was to expand the big wolf pen in time to cover several acres as fencing became available; and there were enough eager volunteers to help install the heavy steel fence in the harsh Rocky Mountain terrain, at 9,200 feet elevation. No easy job, to say the least, and the expansions would take years to complete.

The alpha female of the big wolf pen, Cyndar, was two years old; for the most part, she was reluctant to meet new visitors, but she was excited to see the pups. Cyndar was tall, with long lanky legs and huge feet with big bold toenails. The bottom of her toes and feet were nearly white, a contrast to her rich mahogany black fur. Her muzzle was sprinkled with white and silver markings, and an endearing gaze peered out behind her lovely eyes.

Cyndar was at a perfect age to naturally become alpha mom to the puppies. Little Noya was a real sweetheart and such a little beauty. She was creamy colored with tawny highlights, smaller than the other pups and fragile like a delicate flower. Little Noya struggled with her relationships among the other pups. One day, she walked right into the middle of a dominance brawl between Hota and Mera. She got caught in between the two adults and suffered serious head injuries. The diagnosis from the vet was bleak; she had a fractured skull, and the prognosis was she did not have long to live.

However, if Noya were living as a wild wolf, she would probably die, but Noya survived, and she grew up similar to someone with autism or a nervous system disorder. Little Noya would never be fully respected by any of the other wolves. They tolerated her, but just barely. She was meek and lacked the ability to stand up for herself. She immediately became the scapegoat with any wolf she companioned. For that reason, Noya did not remain very long in the big wolf pack, with the other rough-and-tumble pups. She was separated and moved to a new pen.

Inside the big wolf pen, large ponderosa pine trees loomed over scattered masses of red rocks. All different sizes of rocks, some huge (several tons), sculpted an outcropping at the top of the enclosure that served as a natural overlook for the wolves to see everything going on in the aspen valley. The trees provided great shade from the heat of the summer sun and kept the ground in the lowest part of the valley cool. Many dead trees had fallen throughout the hilly terrain; they also provided shade, shelter, and a place to play. At the highest point in the big wolf pen, a small plateau ran up a hill and across a ravine, ending at the fence right behind a large, dead tree. Across from this upper corner of the enclosure, visitors could walk and observe the wolves during daylight hours. Visitors often watched the wolves watch them.

The wet summer brought out the best in the little valley the wolves called home. Scrub oak, rabbit brush, and sagebrush filled the grounds with a pastel palette, highlighted by the emerald greens of the local wild grass. A small spring ran through the base of the big wolf pen, creating two small ponds before it then trailed out and ran down to the next enclosure. The ponds were just big enough for the wolves to get a drink or play in, like a kiddy wading pool. They liked to wrestle with each other in the spring ponds. In the farthest corner of the big wolf pen, away from people, was a point where the fence came the closest to one of the biggest trees at the sanctuary; the wolves seemed to feel especially comfortable there.

Set like a stage in a large theater, only on nature's floor, this was a surreal, almost magical place for the wolves to be; it was here that Cyndar choose to dig her den. The females were separated from the males during the breeding season to prevent new litters, but they would still go through varying degrees of pseudo-pregnancy. Each spring, even though she was not pregnant, Cyndar went through the emotions and physical symptoms as if she were. False pregnancy creates physical changes in a female wolf, including the urge to den up. Females are driven to dig a den in the spring. Cyndar choose a den site in the enclosure that was far enough away from people, making it easy for her to go about daily life without interruption.

Each spring, Cyndar would revamp or add to her den, digging farther and farther back. At that time, no one at the sanctuary realized just how special the den site would become to the wolves. Many different wolves came to use the den. Cyndar would go into burrowing mode, a few weeks after her estrus cycle usually in February and be digging into March. In a perfect wolf world, she would bear a litter after a short gestation period. Although she had not mated, her mind, her emotions, and her body tricked her into believing she was pregnant.

With all the emotional intensity, if Cyndar did have pups, her instincts would tell her to nurse them. And she would need to protect her vulnerable infants for several weeks, until they wandered out of the den on their own. Cyndar would not allow the other wolves inside the den during the height of her hormonal swing. She defended the den against both wolves and people with loud warning growls and snarls. She was in no mood for visiting of any kind during this time. As a replacement to her pups, Cyndar was given a small stuffed toy. She used to cuddle and lick the toy, keeping it close to her, tucked up where her pups would be.

By the time the summer heat hit, Cyndar would come out of her false pregnancy and generally return to her usual outgoing self.

During that time all the wolves could use the den as a cool retreat. And even though other wolves used it, it was Cyndar that had done most of the work, clearing out the den and enlarging it. When the time was right, Cyndar would again defend it as hers.

CHAPTER 5

The Story of Rowdy

You can take the wolf out of nature, but you cannot take the nature out of the wolf!

Rowdy was a huge, 126-pound white male wolf, born at a roadside zoo in Colorado. As a puppy he was sold as a wolf-dog cross to a man and his young son as a pet. As a pure wolf, Rowdy could not be legally sold to the public. But if breeders created documents stating Rowdy was 98 percent wolf and 2 percent dog, they could bypass any legal problem. Rowdy moved with his man and boy to Texas.

The boy did not live with the wolf and his dad full time. He lived with his mother during the school season and stayed with his father in the summer. After many months away, the boy returned to visit his dad and see Rowdy. Without thinking anything of it, the boy went into Rowdy's enclosure unsupervised. The boy did not realize the wolf was ready to play with an intensity he had not experienced before. Rowdy had grown much larger since the boy had last seen him, and once inside Rowdy's cage, the boy became overwhelmed by the excited wolf. Rowdy remembered playing with the boy's shoes, grabbing at his feet and legs, like he did as a pup. At his size and strength a year later, the young wolf's advances scared the boy; this in turn caused Rowdy to become much more aggressive.

The boy's screams brought Dad running out, and Rowdy became more possessive when he saw his owner head towards them. Rowdy's intensity escalated, and he grabbed the boy's leg; Rowdy picked him up and tried to carry him away from his father. When Dad advanced to help his son, Rowdy bit down hard on the boy's leg, growling as he held on firmly. Once Dad got hold of the wolf, he used all his strength to physically pry the animal's mouth open and lift the wolf off his son. Rowdy was still young, an adolescent, very much like the boy; luckily, the owner did not respond to this incident by having him euthanized.

Rowdy did not have the full physical size of a mature, adult male wolf, or it could have been much worse. He was quickly growing and evolving way beyond any dog cross. The incident was a real eye-opener, and the father recognized that his dream to keep a wolf as a pet had turned into a nightmare. The boy suffered physical injuries to his legs that required stitches, and he was plagued by nightmares after the incident. Rowdy's wild behavior caused him to lose his home with a compassionate owner who would otherwise have done anything to care for the animal throughout its lifetime. And the boy lost a part of his childhood to nightmares that caused him to relive the very traumatic incident for some time afterwards.

For the next year, Rowdy's owner kept him at his job site, where he lived on a concrete cement pad. When his owner could no longer keep the wolf, he loaded Rowdy into a travel trailer and made the long, grueling road trip back to Colorado. In transport, a terrified Rowdy continuously tried to escape as they traveled down the highway, biting and tearing open holes in the walls and roof of the trailer. After many stops to repair the trailer, they finally made it to Mission: Wolf (stressed out and just by the hair on Rowdy's chinny, chin, chin). Rowdy had gone from being sold as a part dog pup from a family roadside zoo to living as a pure wolf in Texas on a concrete pad away from people. Now a few years later, he returned to Colorado and a new home in the mountains, a wilderness habitat unlike anything the wolf had seen before.

Rowdy's habitat was located at the base of the valley running through the sanctuary. A small spring pond formed at the roots of a huge tree. Steep hills were loaded with aspen trees; many had fallen and were now dead on the ground. Rocks, grass, and foliage covered the ground in between the well-worn paths that led in and out of the trees and across the valley to the other side. The new arrival was disoriented in his new lush habitat; the big wolf literally stumbled, falling over the dead trees and rocks in the enclosure, bruising his legs as he went tumbling down the steep hill. Occasionally, Rowdy's original owner would visit. When he did, Kent would go inside the enclosure with him and Rowdy.

Whenever Kent visited Rowdy, the big wolf would jump up on him, putting his front feet on Kent's shoulders. Rowdy was so tall that if he wanted to, he could rest his chin on the top of Kent's head. Kent estimated he measured six feet from tip of tail to tip of nose. Shortly before I arrived, Mission: Wolf had taken Rowdy in as a full-time resident. But I had little interest in going into the enclosure with Rowdy. It was not only that he was huge and very intimidating. His story was fresh in my mind; he learned to hurt a person, and I did not trust him.

CHAPTER 6

Learning the Wolf Language

I did not fear walking Shaman; I feared my inadequacy as a two-legged human to keep up with him and any problem that may arise from that.

After a short time living around the wolves, I began to develop bonds with several of them. Lucus, Mera, Noya, Cyndar, and Nikkolah were really curious about me. During visits inside the wolf enclosures, Kent began to notice how well the wolves took to me. It felt very natural to be around them as if I were already a member of the pack. I welcomed all opportunities to learn from them. Kent encouraged me to spend more time working with the wolves, especially the fearful, shy, elusive, or stubborn ones (that was pretty much all of them). I noticed right off, it seemed the wolves were straight out and direct with their communications toward each other and toward me.

If I did not get into the enclosure and kneel down by the time they reached me to say hello, they would run up to greet and investigate me by jumping up slamming their front paws on to my shoulders. They were especially rambunctious and competed with one another to get to my face first. The two alpha wolves, Cyndar and Lucus, usually reached me ahead of the others. They would always jump up to check out my mouth first. Often with quite a force, the wolves would land with their paws on my shoulders or back; sometimes this would catch me off-guard or send me backwards or sideways. My reward for such greetings would be big slobbering kisses on my cheek and lips. Sometimes I got a painful lip pinch that resulted in a bloody or a fat lip. The mouthy greetings were overwhelming, something that would take me some time to get used to.

As I watched the wolves, face-to-face was generally the first greeting they would give each other. Whether it was a person or another wolf, everyone got a mouth-to-mouth inspection. Sitting down on a rock or log or even the ground and being on the same level as the wolves made them feel more at ease and curious to approach new people. It also, at least most of the time, prevented the wolves from jumping up on people who were not quite prepared. The wolves would hang around for a specific amount of time, always short visits, and no one could determine how long that would be or do anything to change it. The wolves had more important things to do, so when they were done, off they would go. The wolves had no need to just hang around soliciting attention or trying to be petted like a dog.

As the months passed by, Shaman became more and more comfortable with me. I just stood back and did not push myself on him. I ignored him when he ignored me, and big news: he began allowing me to scratch him. His fur was magnificent and was well worth the wait to touch. I started to learn to walk with Shaman, holding his lead briefly here and there, with Kent always nearby in case of a problem. Whenever we traveled to present the wolf program and teach people about wolves in the wild, the challenges captive wolves faced and empathize the importance of preserving wilderness habitat, Lakoda accompanied Shaman. Having a friendly dog along helped calm the intense wolf in a way neither Kent nor I could replicate. This made life slightly easier, but it did not curb his wild personality entirely. For most of the first year working in the Ambassador wolf program, I would handle Lakoda and watched Kent with Shaman.

I had a lot of fun with Lakoda and felt safe and comfortable with him, but I was curious and really wanted to learn to handle Shaman. Kent encouraged me to do more work with Shaman, thinking this could help bring him out of his shy shell. More and more, Kent would briefly hand Shaman's leash over to me during exercise time; this intimated me at first. Into Shaman's second year, his personality began to clearly change; he became more intense and testy with Kent and Lakoda. Shaman was growing bigger and stronger and more independent. I was developing quite a bond with him. All I learned and experienced excited me, and I used every opportunity to strengthen my own confidence. I felt I needed to step up and try to be responsible for handling Shaman myself, without help from Kent. We talked about me taking Shaman on walks around the sanctuary grounds. This sounded like a great idea at the time, and I thought it would be just the thing Shaman and I needed to bring us even closer.

I did not fear walking Shaman; I feared my inadequacy as a two-legged human to keep up with him and any problem that may arise from that. I briefly took hold of Shaman's leash. Kent was standing right there, holding Shaman tight. He seemed reluctant to hand over the big wolf's leash to me, trying to explain just how strong Shaman was. I nodded, believing I understood that walking Shaman on a leash was much different than walking Lakoda. We started running on the sand. I felt the leash tighten up and pull me forward faster. I tightened my grip on the leash handle but quickly realized that I was holding on for dear life.

Anxiety roared up within me as I felt myself being pulled to the maximum speed my legs could physically run. If I jumped forward in strides, instead of trying to run, Shaman would pull me ahead. My feet seemed to touch down in the sand every ten feet. It turned out that yelling only made the wolf move faster; I quickly learned that the wolf did not respond to voice commands when he was lost in a state of pure abandon. I used my body as an anchor and tried to dig my feet into the sand. That backfired too and turned into a kind of tug-of-war: who could pull harder, the wolf or the human?

I got a little glimpse of exactly what Kent meant by the strength of a wolf on a leash.

I did not run Shaman for long that day; I was too afraid that I would lose control and accidentally let go of his leash. I was so intimidated that I quickly handed the leash back to Kent. If Shaman did get loose, he could run too far and too fast to catch. He could easily cover many miles, exploring and looking for food to hunt.

In the wild, it made sense for free roaming wolves to explore away from one another; they check back with their pack mates from time to time, using howl vocalizations to locate one another. The problem was it could be days in between these encounters. By then, a wolf like Shaman loose in a populated area would likely be shot or hit by a car. So as a captive wolf, he was never allowed to free run, except within the safe confines of his enclosure. I could not help but think how wonderful it would be if we could let Shaman free run. Occasionally, Lakoda could free run, because he always chose to stay close to us. Shaman was an entirely different story.

During the brief period I ran Shaman that day, I knew it would take more time working with him to feel comfortable walking and especially running together. We worked for a few months, and then I decided it was time to buckle down and start a routine of walking Shaman on a regular basis, especially around the sanctuary grounds. The big wolf showed complete joy when he was allowed to explore new territory. What better way to share a positive experience with another species of life? One morning, after what seemed like weeks of rain, I had grown tired of putting off our walks, due to poor weather or ground conditions. Motivated to take a risk, I decided I was going to go for it, whether the ground was dry or not; I would be fine. I grabbed Shaman's leash and walked out toward his enclosure. When he saw me coming up the path carrying his chain leash, dangling and clanging together, making a noise he was all too familiar with, he became excited.

As I reached Shaman's entry gate, I slipped my hand through the fence opening and grabbed the latch on the opposite side. I hesitated a few seconds and then slowly started to push open the large gate. Shaman jumped up to greet me with such an explosion of energy it was difficult for me to get inside. I realized it was not the greatest timing to go inside his enclosure; I decided to stand quietly at the gate for a few moments and wait for Shaman to settle his energy down. Once Shaman became bored and lost interest with me standing outside the gate, he moved away and ran to the opposite side of his pen to show off to the other wolves. I saw my opportunity and hurriedly opened the gate and stepped in.

Inside Shaman's enclosure, the atmosphere was quite different. Shaman immediately came running over to me. Making noise with his mouth gaping open and tongue flopping as he ran, he proceeded to run circles around me. Shaman used his nose to touch the lead rope of his leash, as if to say, "Let's go!" He made his usual squeaks of excitement but also made high-pitched sounds I had never heard before. Intriguing new sounds. I was not quick enough to grab hold and stop him the first time he came running by; he was so excited and was moving to fast. Shaman lived in an enclosure next to Rowdy, who seemed to be a big rival to Shaman's wolf manliness, I guess. Nothing gave Shaman a bigger charge than to show off to Rowdy. My cold fingers were slowing me down. It took a few minutes for me to gather up the chain and organize it enough to successfully get it around his neck.

The two rival male wolves ran along the boundary of their enclosures, challenging one another with their body language. I rolled my eyes back in my head at the two, so much like human boys rivaling over one another. Shaman held his tail high, waving it in the air at Rowdy like a flag. His guard hair stood straight up on end, hackled from the top of his head to the tip of his tail. It seemed that even though I was standing there holding a leash, Shaman was more interested in challenging the big white wolf. Rowdy did not help much either. He was inviting Shaman to the opposite hill; all puffed up like a big white marshmallow. His long platinum guard hairs jumped around his neckline as he moved. It was clear as I watched the body language between the two wolves that Shaman and Rowdy would likely fight if they had the chance.

My cold hands struggled, and with a shaky confidence I reached to grab hold of Shaman and get the leash around his neck. My fingers again fumbled the chain. I felt clumsy and uncoordinated, and this encouraged the wolf to not take me seriously. Already my job of catching Shaman was challenged simply by the addition of Rowdy's influence. Shaman was not trained like a dog, he had no manners, and he did not know what "sit" meant or stay for that matter. I had to be patient and wait for the next time Shaman passed by. When he did, I swung my arms around him and grabbed the thick fur around his neck. This slowed him almost to a stop, but like an old tractor locked in gear, he kept moving forward. "Pop!" Shaman was free of my grasp and again running back toward the fence line. After several passes and misses on my part, I started to exaggerate my voice. I called Shaman over to me. He came running over happily, clueless that I was having any problem.

I quickly wrapped the chain around his neck. I knew he wanted to run back over toward Rowdy, who continued to entice Shaman by mimicking the big wolf's body language. Shaman pulled against me as I worked to get the clip hooked. Once the chain was hooked, I dropped the leash and let Shaman drag the lead loosely behind him while he did another round of strutting. Now that his lead was on, he seemed to settle down and was looking at me differently, as if I had something important to say. First, I had to double-check the collar link and make sure I had gotten it tight enough around his neck to stay put and not slip over his head.

When I was satisfied that I had the chain on correctly, my nerves started to well up, and my knees became a little weak. Reality faced me as I nervously gathered up the lead and reached up to open the entry gate; I asked myself whether I should really do this. As the gate swung open, Shaman seemed to forget that I was attached to him. He leapt forward, up and out toward the path with such a force that I had to jump to keep up with him. Shaman paused momentarily outside the entrance of his enclosure to grab a quick sniff of the bush outside the gate. I took advantage of this second or two of calmness and regained my balance. I eyed Shaman. His nose went up slightly as he investigated the air.

My plan was to walk up the path behind Shaman's enclosure, beyond Rowdy's enclosure, and hike up the hill behind the sanctuary. Ideally I wanted to avoid any and all contact with other wolves, who would be watching excitedly from inside their enclosures. As I took a few steps out in the direction I intended to go, I quickly realized that Shaman was not following my lead. Suddenly, he turned and ran down the hill toward Rowdy's enclosure. I watched in horror as Shaman passed right by me (as if I was not even there), running back down the hill toward his gate. Did I mention it had been raining? My wet and cold fingers continued to fumble, and I struggled to gain some kind of control in my about-to-be disaster.

I lost control of the direction I was heading and slid off the path as gravity and Rowdy dictated the direction I was heading. I struggled to dodge the trees and rocks as we went down the hill. I believe Shaman knew exactly what kind of train wreck was going on behind him. He ignored me and took advantage of my weakness. As he headed off down the hill toward Rowdy, he became determined, pulling harder with every step he took. He was dragging me behind him like a rag doll.

As we went down the hill, I remember noticing the freshness of the air; the smell was so sweet all around me. The rain had been good to the aspen forest. I was sliding down the hill, out of control, behind a powerful wolf that was dodging trees like a professional ski racer. All I could do was hang on and try not to land head first into a tree or rock. Or let him loose. His grace was offset by my clumsiness. What was I thinking?

I felt like an amateur water skier behind a boat heading into a group of mangrove trees. Instead, I was heading straight for an aspen tree that was as big around as my body, with no rescue boat to turn around and pull me out. Shaman picked up speed, realizing he could now get over face-to-face with Rowdy. His hackles were still standing on end, and his tail was flagging up high in the air. It was if he was shouting out at Rowdy, "Now I am going to kick your butt!" And the closer he got to the big white wolf, the less he noticed the dilemma happening behind him. I was hanging on for dear life, sliding down the hill, not knowing where I was going to end up or if it would be on my feet or on my face.

Instantly, Shaman's focus was broken by a rude jolt when the chain stopped him in his tracks. He went left and I went slightly right of the big tree. The aspen stopped us both. I could see Shaman bounce backwards slightly and stop. I flinched as I realized that my finger got smashed and pinned under the chain against the tree. It was my finger that took the brunt of the collision with the tree. I winced in pain, as I looked down at my sad red hand, now pinned up against the bark of the tree. My right index finger felt and looked broken. Sharp pain went through my entire hand as I hurried to free my finger.

I felt disappointment at myself and quickly regretted the decision to take Shaman out of his enclosure without Kent's help. Shaman, however, did not even flinch. I watched as he kept his focus on Rowdy, his energy going in a forward momentum to challenge the big white wolf. Shaman stood still for a few seconds, just long enough for me to act. Without giving it any thought, I grabbed up the slack of the rope and wrapped it around the trunk of the tree. I intended to use the tree for leverage that would take the pressure off my hands. I hurried with my free hand and managed to pull enough slack from the chain to get my finger free.

I leaned over to regain my balance, and with Shaman still tethered to the tree, I sat down for a few seconds to catch my breath. I tried to hold back my tears, but I could not help it, feeling betrayed by my wolf friend. I pulled Shaman back up the hill toward me, using my injured hand as an anchor to the tree and my free hand to tow him slowly back up the hill with the chain. I believed once I got his attention away from Rowdy's influence, I could get him back to his enclosure. I had it! That was the end of that walk. I looked around at my surroundings and thought it would be wise to use the terrain as my aids. Trees, bushes, and even rocks became my stops, grabs, and balancers.

I was worried that Shaman would have no respect for me; after all, I believed that Shaman could see my inability to handle him, and he took advantage of the fact. I exhibited a display of complete weakness. I realized I would have to think about that later; at that moment, I had to focus on what was at hand. Shaman again was pulling against me, toward Rowdy. I continued to hold pressure on his chain for several moments. I waited until he released back toward me, even if it was only a footstep. It took some patience on my part, and finally he turned back up toward me. Shaman was clearly in his own world, the potential of challenging his rival sent him out of his body.

In this case, Shaman appeared to be in a blind pursuit, not really aware of his surroundings, and I could tell where I ranked on his scale of hierarchy; literally, my rank was non-existent. As I towed Shaman back up to the path from tree to bush, Rowdy continued to taunt him. Shaman found it nearly impossible to ignore the big wolf's gestures and presence. What a way to spoil the fun of the adventure. I thought in hindsight the momentum of Shaman's pull, combined with the slippery nature of the ground, made for a complete accident waiting to happen. I should have seen the seriousness of this before I put the leash on Shaman's neck. Lesson learned! Or was it?

The reality, and maybe it was hard for me to hear at the time, was that the mud was only part of the reason I could not control Shaman. The main reason was his complete lack of respect for me. Many years later, this would come back to haunt me; I would grow to understand just how important it was to earn the respect of the wolf I was working with. I was determined to handle these animals with grace. But at that moment, I wondered how I could learn to get respect from an animal like Shaman? Was there a way to communicate with him that did not include physical abuse, food deprivation, or isolation? Handling Shaman was a challenge, but I was not about to resort to abuse on any level. These ways pained my heart. What felt right was to follow my heart, to be natural and honest with the animals and with myself.

I loved challenging my intuition, using inner guidance to help me when I needed it, no matter for what. And my instincts seemed healthy, feeling as if they waited ready to spring at a second's notice if needed. Shaman's mind always seemed to be three steps ahead of mine. I quickly learned that I had to change everything I thought I knew about understanding canines in order to better understand Shaman. I began to sense how Shaman wanted to be treated, and my saving grace would be doing just that sensing how to behave around him. With no outside aid or resources to help me understand him, I would fall back on my instincts and intuition time and time again. I had to learn to control my outbursts and temper tantrums around the wolves; now it was about awareness, self-control, and patience in addition to instinct and intuition for survival amongst the wolf pack.

It was really mind over matter for me, learning the opposite of what I had been previously taught about canines, about life. Wolves are sensitive, fickle creatures. Many times, figuring out Shaman was like putting my hand on a hot stove; I knew as the temperature rose that if I did not back off and let him cool down, I could get burned.

Instead, I turned my focus inward on myself. I became aware of just how much subtle body language put pressure on Shaman. Small things that I took for granted in the beginning and paid no mind to would often make him uncomfortable. And when I would look away or physically back away from him, opening up space between us, I could see him relax and react positively and step with me, not away from me. I did not know what I was doing wrong that brought on his tension; all I knew was the more I worked with Shaman, the more I wanted to work with him, even if it meant a few broken bones along the way.

CHAPTER 7

Walking Nikkolah

Nikkolah was a powerhouse of potential in all directions, a guardian of free will, and he had proven himself time and time again.

Nikkolah was a rather large (around one hundred pounds) wolf with a thick, stocky build and stout legs; he was feral in nature even though he was raised in captivity. He looked like a powerhouse of raw strength and had a personality that danced to the beat of his own drum. With sandy brown fur, tipped in black and white mixed throughout, he looked exactly like a gray wolf from any book or magazine. At least that's what I thought when I first met him. Nikkolah's head was huge; his face was long, flat and narrow, with a strong, dignified snout.

Although he had yellow eyes, as all wolves do, they did not pop with the same intensity as they would against black fur. Still, they flashed in the sun.

Nikkolah was skittish around new people; when I first arrived at the sanctuary, I was able to get a lot of hands-on time and contact with him, and we developed a bond. He was a curious fellow around me and seemed to accept me even easier and quicker than Shaman initially did. Nikkolah enjoyed having his back, neck, and head scratched. He did a sort of body shake when my fingers hit the right spot on the center of his back. He would bring up his rear leg tightly underneath him and kick away, twisting his body to keep his balance. He held his head up as if he had transcended the sensations of the scratches and was floating above his body. Ears pinned, he tightened his lips, and his whole being reacted. Nikkolah was a powerhouse of potential in all directions, a guardian of free will, and he had proven himself time and time again. At three years old, he continued to try to escape his enclosure and explore the other wolf pens.

Nikkolah had never gotten over his ability to freely move from enclosure to enclosure, as he had during puppyhood. After a short time living with Cyndar and Lucus, he seemed bored; unlike the other wolves, Nikkolah did not see the chain link fence as a limitation. It was really Nikkolah who was responsible for molding Kent and several others into fence-building experts. It took a lot of labor and creativity to contain one determined master escape artist wolf. For a young wolf, he had, in a very short time, created quite a reputation for himself. He had a very headstrong and mischievous personality, which earned him the nickname "Tricky Nikki" due to his somewhat trickster nature. Nikkolah worked the fence in as many different ways as he could come up with, seeking any way to get out.

Nikkolah had a knack for finding little holes or loose wire in the main structure of the enclosure. This became a daily occurrence for Nikkolah. The determined wolf pulled on wire with his teeth or stretched it with his powerful paws. For him, where there was a will, there was a way. Nikkolah could also climb trees and, like a lion in the Serengeti, look out over his domain. He would be seen frequenting the thickest and heaviest branches of the old ponderosa pine tree at the entrance gate of the big wolf pen, watching curiously what the people in the parking lot were doing and what was happening with his neighboring wolf companions. He even went as far as to be seen scaling across the top edge of the chain link fence, grasping the wire with his thick paws.

Although there were many attempts, Nikkolah only actually got out of the big wolf pen a couple of times. He did not run away or try to leave the sanctuary property, as one might expect. Instead, he went around to the outside of the other wolf enclosures, curious to get up close to his neighboring wolves, until he reached Rowdy's enclosure. There, for some reason known only to him, he decided to climb in with the big white wolf. Surprisingly, Rowdy accepted this new visitor—at least at first. Kent said it seemed Nikkolah was having trouble deciding which enclosure he wanted to be in. After his most recent climb-in with Rowdy, Nikkolah was left to live there, assuming it was his choice. Six months later, the two males began to heat up and start fighting. Since the two were not getting along, I wondered why Nikkolah wasn't trying to climb the fence again.

One day, I walked up to the enclosure and stood outside, studying the recent improvements to the fence line. Rowdy's fence was a bit too much to climb from the inside out, even for Nikkolah. It could have been due to a slight over hang at the top of the fence. One thin strand of electric wire stretched the perimeter of the fence line top and may well have kept Nikkolah from making any escape attempts. Or perhaps it was because the fence was built in the aspen tree ravine, making the terrain too steep to climb out of. We did not know, all we knew was as each day passed, Rowdy and Nikkolah fought more frequently, with heightened intensity.

The aggression between the two wolves was putting pressure on us to get Nikkolah out and move him back down the hill to the big wolf pen, before one of the wolves got hurt. The question was how. We could tranquilize him or try to crate him; both options had potential side effects. It would be easiest if one of us could leash him and walk him back down to the big wolf pen.

Growing up, Nikkolah had always been the more dominant of all the pups, including Lucus. But back in the big wolf pen, Raven, Jordan, and Cyndar were treating Lucus, the ghost-eyed black beauty, like he was the leader of the pack. Lucus had stepped up to the role of alpha male by default, in Nikkolah's absence. It would be interesting to see if Lucus's pack would even accept Nikkolah back. Then the question arose as what to do if they did not accept him. We would cross that bridge when we reached it. It had been some time since I last had an opportunity to be one-on-one with Nikkolah due to my healthy respect of Rowdy.

Kent felt that if he tried to move Nikkolah, the wolf would become too nervous, and the two would end up in a wreck. But seeing that I had developed a friendship or bond with Nikkolah, Kent thought I could put a leash on his neck and walk him down the hill to the big wolf pen.

When the day came to make the move, we decided it would be best that anyone volunteering at the sanctuary while I had Nikkolah on the leash would stay inside the community building and watch from the windows. Including Kent. That was to insure no one could accidentally scare Nikkolah. And although I was grateful that others were looking out for me, I was more insecure about becoming a show. I was wearing purple and blue tie-dyed leggings; really, they were long underwear but with the bright colors, who could tell the difference? They were lightweight and allowed me to move freely as I walked; I often ran in them. With that, I had my heavy hiking boots on and finished my "walking Nikkolah" outfit off with a sweatshirt, to help protect my arms in case the walk took an unexpected turn.

Kent reminded me about what happened with Shaman, a memory I would not soon forget, and warned me to be ready for Nikkolah's strength and nervous edge. Nikkolah would be much worse to handle, because it had been a while since he had walked on a lead. As I thought about it, this indeed would be more challenging than walking Shaman. Regardless, I felt like I could catch, leash, and walk him; after all, what could go wrong? Could it be worse than what happened with Shaman? My hand still hurt from that. My own reasoning was—if I was going to truly help the wolves live at the sanctuary, some of them could potentially have a future being walked on a leash. Maybe the ones like Nikkolah just needed a reminder of what it was like to wear a leash and be out somewhere new, tethered to a person.

Ready to try walking Nikkolah, I gathered up the chain and collar that Kent gave me to use. As I headed up the hill in the direction of Rowdy's enclosure, I realized just how much of the walk was going to be down hill, some places steeper than others, and parts with lots of loose gravel. My stomach churned as I became nervous. My mind reeled with what ifs and what to dos. *I need to make sure to keep myself safe once I get the collar secured around his neck,* I thought to myself. I dangled the chain made from small, thin, and smooth links that served as the lead. It was attached to a larger link chain collar Kent had made.

As I neared the enclosures, both wolves saw me coming and excitedly ran to the entrance gate of their pen. Shaman was running around at the perimeter of his enclosure, too, thinking he was going for a walk. The first thing I could see was all of them wagging their tails as they squeaked like happy puppies. I opened the perimeter gate, a wooden and chain link gate leading into a small visiting space, with a bench to sit on, and closed the gate behind me. I paused and watched Rowdy and Nikkolah run past the gate; it looked like they both were thinking they were about to get out. As I stood waiting for the energy to calm down, I looked up at Shaman; he had a confused look on his face, like he could not imagine what I was up to, standing inside another wolf enclosure with a lead in my hand. I waited a moment longer and rested my hand on the gate latch, and as soon as Rowdy was far enough away and Nikkolah was right there, that was when I wanted to act.

The second Rowdy was distracted by the other wolves, I quickly and without hesitation opened the gate. Nikkolah, seeing the opportunity, quickly darted into the perimeter with me. I slammed the gate shut behind Nikkolah; he barely got his tail and body through before Rowdy caught on and came running. Excited to be in a new space, Nikkolah jumped around in the small square of the double entry gate in sheer joy. He was happy to see me as he wagged his tail, but he was also interested in smelling the new territory. Rowdy hit the fence opposite of Nikkolah, puffed up, white hackles standing on end; Rowdy's sheer massive presence startled me and blew me away. His guard hair looked at least six inches tall off his shoulders, running down his neck along his back and to his tail.

I half fell backwards down on to the bench; the slam caught me off-guard and caused me to doubt my ability to handle the situation. I was again reminded how powerful these animals were. The reality of the risk I was about to take began to set in. I decided to sit back on the bench a moment longer and take a breath, regain my balance and composure. Nikkolah stood smelling the deck, still wagging his tail. I took a few moments to rub his back. My adrenaline fired, and it was hard for me to calm myself down enough for the wolves to calm down too. Rowdy ran another big circle away from the gate; the big wolf came running back over and again slammed into the gate, his way of saying he wanted to join us. This behavior agitated me. I worked to focus my attention on Nikkolah and ignore Rowdy.

After all, it was good to see Nikkolah again and handle him. I realized how much I missed not being able to go into the enclosure with him because I was too afraid of Rowdy. I noticed he had really grown. I reassured myself that I was off to a good start by getting Nikkolah in the holding pen without letting Rowdy out. I felt sure that had I slipped and accidentally done that, I would be sitting in (or under) the middle of a fight. And although Rowdy was not afraid of me, was curious and even solicited attention from me, I cannot deny that Rowdy made me nervous. It was hard to hide that kind of fear. I knew he had hurt someone before, and I could not help believing it would be easy for him to hurt someone again. Especially someone like me, I did not know Rowdy as a bonded pack member, like I did Nikkolah, so in a sense I was a rival of Rowdy's too.

As Nikkolah was busy eagerly smelling the bench and the ground around my feet, checking out the inside of the holding pen, I reached down to attach the collar around his neck. It was easy for me to do because he was so engrossed in the smells; he barely noticed

I did anything. I took my time to clip the chain on the right setting. Putting the collar on Nikkolah was the easy part. It was when I walked him outside that things got much more interesting. When he realized the outer gate, leading out to the big, wide world, was open, he bolted out with a jerk.

He pulled me with such force it smashed my hand up against the gate as I charged out behind him, trying to keep up. It was just a bruise, nothing like when I had hurt it walking Shaman in the mud. Nikkolah began to pull me up the hill toward the path, but in the opposite direction of where I wanted to go. As he pulled my body weight up onto the path, his enthusiasm to be out of Rowdy's enclosure dimmed as he briefly turned around and realized I was attached to him. He looked at me with panic in his eyes as he stopped briefly, wondering what I was up to. I realized I was following him to close. I was almost right over the top of his back. I did not have a choice, because the chain was only seven feet long.

He looked at me with fear on his face as I started to run up behind him. I tried to move to the side, but he was too strong and too forceful. That's when everything changed. Nikkolah bolted out and away from me in fear, with a hurricane force that I had never felt before. I had no idea what I did wrong. Nikkolah was stronger and more unpredictable than I had experienced with Shaman. It felt like the power of twenty big dogs, all pulling me at one time.

Another experience of how powerful and out of control a wolf could really become in a moment's notice. As if it were pulled from my memory banks, the scenario began to replay itself. Nikkolah turned and headed back down toward Rowdy's enclosure. In a heartbeat, I lost my balance and found myself head first, falling down the hill behind him. That really freaked him out. As I hit the ground, I lost my grip on the leash. In the blink of an eye, the chain handle flung out of my hand with such a blow it pulled me farther down the hill. I will always remember watching as Nikkolah went from rocketing up the hill to rocketing back down the hill.

Then Nikkolah ran for safety and familiarity up behind Rowdy's enclosure, the leash dragging along behind him and bouncing over the bushes as he went. I was stunned but felt thankful I did not get seriously injured. I was embarrassed and tried to get up quickly; I looked around to see if Kent was watching and pretended nothing happened. But Nikkolah was loose, not running away thank goodness, but running back to Rowdy's enclosure.

He reached the fence and had a little reunion with Rowdy. The two were quiet for a second, but then Nikkolah blurted out a loud roar at the puffed-up, emotional Rowdy, who in turn bared his teeth and roared through the fence right back at Nikkolah. In essence, it seemed that Nikkolah was teasing Rowdy, who was growing more pissed that Nikkolah was out free running around his enclosure and he was not. The two changed directions and began to run back toward me.

Nikkolah seemed to have forgotten all about what just happened; he was so fired up challenging Rowdy, it was as if he had gained some new status or something, running in the free world. I saw the chance to fix the mistake I had made and acted as quickly as I could. I moved down the ravine and back up the hill behind Rowdy's enclosure and up toward Nikkolah. He did not see me climbing up the hill below him. I stopped right up next to the fence in the direction they were heading. I grabbed onto a nearby tree for leverage and balance and pushed myself down into the ground. I saw that I only had a brief window of opportunity to step down hard on the chain that continued to drag behind Nikkolah as he ran past me.

With as much force as I could muster, I stamped down hard and pinned the chain to the ground with my heavy hiking boot. Success was mine! Nikkolah came to an abrupt stop.

There was a good reason to wear the big boots, after all. I would have preferred to walk in shoes or better yet barefoot. In reality, if I had been barefoot, I might not have stood a chance on the leash with this wolf. I grabbed the leash off the ground and firmly held resistance to Nikkolah's pull.

Once he stopped, I gave it all my might to pull him back toward me, again a repeat of the previous experience with Shaman and for the same reason: to get away from a large roaring Rowdy. For a moment, the pressure on his neck from the collar took his mind off the other wolves surrounding us and put his attention on me. He seemed to have forgotten all about my maneuver, or perhaps he was so in his own world he did not even notice that anything happened at all. Forget that I landed on my head and shoulder on the rocky ground behind him and made quite a branch-breaking, stick-crunching racket. In that moment, I realized I needed to get very serious and take a far firmer approach to handling Nikkolah or I was heading for trouble. Perhaps the change of my attitude gave me enough confidence to step up stronger after falling. I moved away from the tree and started hiking my way back toward the path, holding pressure on the chain lead as I went.

From then on, the trees provided me with a security, something that I could ground myself to, grabbing the trunk or a solid thick branch or even a nearby piece of fence to keep or regain my balance. I could feel Nikkolah tense up and start to pull harder when the neighboring wolves challenged him from a distance en route to the big wolf pen. They saw us coming and ran along their fence lines, tails flagging. If I had let him, Nikkolah would have charged to their fences and engaged any and all the other wolves. I held a strong pressure on the lead as I led him in the direction of the big wolf pen. I begin to relax as we went along and fell into a reasonable trot. Nikkolah started to listen; he must have remembered how it felt to be on the leash with a collar around his neck. And I was not fumbling behind him, I was walking next to him, and it felt good.

As we rounded the corner at the top of the parking lot, directly above where everyone was waiting inside the community building, Nikkolah seemed to remember this was where people were usually present. He became more aware. I could feel him tense up, and although all was quiet and there was no sign of movement, he started to dart back and forth nervously at the top of the hill, searching for anything to be scared of. I stopped him and paused, looking around and plotting the last part of the short journey. Nikkolah stood frozen with his legs braced and tail tucked. I saw Kent standing inside the door; I could see by the look on his face that he wanted to somehow help but knew it was best to stay put.

I liked the idea of going zigzag back and forth down the hill. I felt I could keep my composure even if we got running really fast, if I broke up the direction I was headed. I worked to direct Nikkolah back and forth with me as we started to gain speed traveling down the hill. We ran passed the community trailer. Out of the corner of my eye, I could see people standing inside the window, watching. I felt a twinge of nerves come up in me but tried to ignore the feelings and focus back to Nikkolah. They watched me until we were near the entrance of the big wolf pen.

One more steep stretch, and we would reach the gate. I had run out of trees or fence posts to grab hold of. I was on my own and decided to go with it. I watched ahead, scouting every step I hoped to take for pitfalls. I continued to hold as much pressure on the leash as I could. I felt Nikkolah suddenly realize where he was going and accelerate his speed. With every step I took, I dug my boot heals down into the ground. Using the force of all of my weight against Nikkolah's pull, I managed to keep my balance and stay upright. It was hard work to get Nikkolah to zigzag instead of run straight down. When he remembered where we were going, he hit rocket power boosters.

I cannot imagine what it must have looked like to the people inside the building, but it must have been comical. To watch someone be pulled beyond one's physical capacity to move, like hitting the fast forward button on a video. But for me, I did the best I could. Nikkolah had become so excited to get back to see Lucus and the rest of the pack, I could hardly contain my steps over his enthusiasm. It had been months since the wolves had contact with one another, other than vocal howling from a distance. Once we reached the gate, he slowed down. I was able to regain a walk and quickly moved ahead of him to open the gate entrance.

Kent opened the door and stepped out onto the porch. Nikkolah heard the door open and stopped, pausing to look back up the hill at Kent (who had managed to snap a photo capturing the journey). Lucus, Raven, Jordan, and Cyndar were screaming with excitement as we approached, jumping up on the opposite side of the gate. With a huge sigh of relief, I got the gate opened and Nikkolah safely through, inside with Lucus. Every wolf eagerly accepted Nikkolah's return with happiness, wagging tails, and excited face licks and chewing. I even got greetings of excitement from the pack.

I unclipped Nikkolah's chain and released him back where he belonged. To ensure his containment in the big wolf pen and make sure that he stayed put in the future, a significant amount of work had been done to enhance the big wolf pen during his absence. My heart was pounding with relief that I had made it without embarrassing myself in front of the others.

I dusted off my pants and found that I had scrapped my elbow and knee, oh well, I still felt accomplished. I stood watching as the wolf pack chased Nikkolah around the large enclosure in some kind of reuniting celebration. Squealing with excitement, Nikkolah bowed down immediately with his body language, showing his admiration and acceptance of Lucus's kingly status. Nikkolah was running around after Lucus, who growled and repeatedly bit Nikkolah's nose; it was clear that Lucus was alpha, and that was okay with Nikkolah. In fact, he seemed relieved to be back. Kent and the others walked down, and together we watched as the wolves rejoiced. I acknowledged to myself a job well done, for sticking with it after I fell down the hill and not letting my fear override my ability to get over a potentially dangerous situation, regardless of a few scrapes, bumps and bruises.

Walking Nikkolah to the big wolf pen.
Photograph courtesy Kent Weber, 1989.

CHAPTER 8

"Baaahhh!" Says the Wolf

Hugging Shaman was out of the question. It was as if the wolf did not know what to do with the energy and emotion of a human hug that it was too much for him.

Several months during the year, we travelled in a van to present programs with Shaman and Lakoda. Lakoda had a couple of places he liked to sleep during the long hours driving. Shaman was very busy mentally. He rarely napped in the van; instead, he looked out the window or chewed on bones. Most of all, he just wanted to watch what was going on. Traveling with Lakoda was a calming and gentle influence on Shaman. However, it did not solve all his temperamental quirks. I remember thinking how nice it would be if Shaman took on a lot of the dog's mannerisms. Time would tell; in the meantime, we were experiencing quite the opposite of Lakoda's dog behaviors.

Shaman had a lot of opinions, and he had no problem sharing those views in a very boisterous and intense voice. I learned early on as our friendship developed that he was a very hands-off kind of wolf. Too bad; it was hard not to reach out and stroke his gorgeous fur, especially since I grew up with different dogs that wanted constant attention, to the point of frequent annoyance. A few times, I would catch myself automatically reaching out to pet Shaman as if he were one of those canines. One day as we drove down the highway, someone left a mess on the floor, and I knelt down to start cleaning it. When I moved back toward Shaman, I sat down on the bench right next to him. He was apprehensive of my pushing myself into his space, but I did the best I could to ignore him and continue to clean.

Once I got the mess cleaned up and in the bag, I stashed it under the seat for later disposal; without hesitation, I reached out and touched Shaman's thick neck. This forward movement on my part apparently caught him off-guard; it happened so fast, and his immediate reaction was classic: "Baaahhh!" A deep guttural roar came easily and naturally out of his flashy, toothy pie-hole. The energy blast sent me slightly backwards and down. My reaction was probably predictable. It scared the living daylights out of me; ha! That would teach me to try to pet him.

It was the perfect "Baaahhh" sound, followed by a jump up onto his feet and a look that matched the sound coming from his mouth. It was as if Shaman scolded or yelled at me for touching him. His "Baaahhh" made the hair stand up on the back of my neck. When he was done, he looked to find a new zone where he could settle back down and scan out the window undisturbed. I was beginning to learn there was more to this communication thing than I knew about. To a wolf, petting was a form of communication, beyond the typical affection role it played with our dog friends. Shaman's "Baaahhh" made me aware that I was more like the dog in my need to touch. To Shaman, when Kent leaned over his shoulders to rub him, the wolf perceived Kent was attempting to dominate him. In reality Kent was showing his love for him.

Lakoda was older than Shaman and loved human attention. The dog could sit at my feet for as long as I was willing to pet him. Now I had learned that to touch could be received by the wolves as a way of communication on a different level of language beyond giving and receiving affection. It was more about learning to read body gestures instead of using voice commands. There was so much silent communication that passed between the wolves, it seemed impossible that I would ever understand it even slightly, but I found this intriguing. Lakoda seemed to think he was the alpha over Shaman, and for a time he convinced Shaman that he was the top dog.

As our friendship grew, Shaman became more comfortable with me moving around him, and he even allowed me to start to touch him. I noticed that anytime I would lean over the top of his shoulders, he would have an exaggerated reaction. He would jump away from me; at first I was confused until we recognized that when wolves living in a pack dominate one another, the alpha often jumps up on the others' shoulders and back. To the wolves, the body language was the same whether it was a person or a wolf expressing it. A fleeting thought came to mind, and I realized it made sense to watch and mirror how the wolves behaved with each other. By mirroring, I thought I could take communication between species to a whole new level.

Well-behaved Lakoda listened pretty well and constantly looked to his human friends for reassurance and direction. Shaman rarely listened to people except when it involved food or if he saw the dog listening. Shaman's self-reliant attitude and mysterious intensity fascinated me, but I still had no idea how to understand him. And although he would allow me to look into his eyes, it was usually for only a greeting's brief second. Once that was over, and I tried to look in his eyes, he would evade my gaze and turn away. What we did understand at the time was Shaman acted like he was the alpha over Kent and me; he acted that way a little toward Lakota too.

Accidentally, without even knowing, Shaman's two human role models failed to show the correct wolf behavior of how to be a leader. We had not yet evolved to an understanding of how a true respected alpha leader could lead its pack to safety and survive. Regardless of my thoughts on mirroring, none of this awareness had grounded itself into my subconscious. At that time, I only knew how to appear vulnerable and submissive, simply by being emotionally involved with Kent began to create distress in Shaman. We were heading down the big road of 'Baaahhh!" It would be some time before either Kent or I would fully understand how to handle a dominant wolf personality.

Shaman became a great teacher to everyone he met. His name alone foretold he would be a medicine man to humanity. He made a tremendous impact during his time as an Ambassador wolf. Personally, Shaman influenced me by showing how I could connect better with animals. Even though it would take years to sink in, I started to understand his body language and intent.

Kent loved Shaman; it was obvious in the way he bent over backwards to make everything perfect for the wolf. Also, Kent's influence as another male was a little threatening to the wolf. Regardless, he took very loving care of every little need that animal had. In the long run, however, our behavior with Shaman would come back to haunt us. Our treatment actually backfired, creating the exact opposite of the relationship we had hoped to have. As time passed on, Shaman focused more and more on his need to be dominant toward Kent. It became an almost daily occurrence for Shaman to discipline Kent with a big Baaahhh!

All different kinds and tones of Baaahhh would come from the wolf's mouth. Some of the Baaahhhs would be loud and stern while others would be soft or short. It did not matter the way Shaman chose to Baaahhh; he got my attention every time. What was surprising to me was the way Kent handled the Baaahhhs. He intentionally held his hand still while the wolf would mouth his arms or hands. I thought that took a lot of guts. It took me some time to get used to being disciplined by the big wolf when all I wanted was to give him a big hug.

Hugging Shaman was out of the question. The wolf did not know what to do with the energy and emotion of a human hug; it seemed too much for him. After living with him for more than a year, he finally began to warm up to me. When he began to trust me, he started a behavior that reminded me of a cat. Maybe it was his way of hugging me; I do not know. His feline move consisted of rubbing up against me and pushing his body against my legs; if I were sitting down, he would push his head into me and walk along with his back arched. Slowly and intentionally always holding his tail up like a flag, Shaman would drag his body alongside mine.

I was soon able to rub Shaman freely. He especially enjoyed having his ears rubbed. When I would scratch sensitive areas like his hips or back legs, he often became overstimulated. He would jump around and grab my arm in his teeth, and the inevitable "Baaahhh" would blast out. It was not easy to get over the fear of being bitten, resisting my natural instinct to pull my arm away whenever I felt he was about to discipline me. The wolf could take on the persona of a huge grizzly bear when he wanted to. Kent would often say, "Shaman uses his mouth like we use our hands." He sure did!

I took what Kent said to heart, and after some time I began to get over my fear, but not without setbacks. Kent and others told me it is not the bite that hurts; it's the reaction to it. The immediate pulling away process is what causes the most injury from a dog bite. Whenever I would forget this, Kent reminded me, "It was not if the wolf will discipline you, it was when." I had to go against my very nature of self-preservation. I watched those powerful jaws crush chicken bones like toothpicks, using teeth the size of one of my fingers; how was I supposed to react when those same teeth bit down on my arm? I often found myself pulling my arm away (or trying to). It took a lot of time and more courage than I knew I had to overcome this aspect of working with wolves.

When "Baaahhh" came out of the wolf's mouth, and his discipline was over, to my relief, my arm was fully intact. No holes or even bruises in sight. Shaman had a keen control of the pressure in his jaws, and like a slap on the wrist, this was his warning to respect his personal space and independence. Even though Shaman would grab my arm to discipline me, it was different from being bitten. Over time, Shaman disciplined me less and less often; the more comfortable I became with him teething my arms, the less likely he was to do it. I do not recommend provoking any canine to bite, and I do not have enough experience to understand the dynamics of being bitten. Nor do I plan to get that experience in the future.

Shaman says, "Baaahhh," as he guards his antelope head from pack mates. Photograph by Tracy Ane Brooks, 1990.

CHAPTER 9

Winds of Change

There was a dense, undeniably dark energy present around Cyndar; it was as if she was depressed, and her heart had broken.

I was learning so much taking care of the wolves, interacting with them, and most importantly watching their behaviors and body language. I loved observing the way the wolves treated each other. Their behavior fascinated me; in so many ways, their interactions resembled the way humans treat each other. When I first met young Zephyr, he had just arrived at Mission: Wolf. The little wolf was put in the community building after a long road trip. Inside the building, Zephyr enjoyed the safety of a small bathtub in the shower room. When I would walk back to visit him, he would stare up at me with fear, hiding behind two wide, unblinking amber-colored eyes. It was apparent by the look in the little wolf's eyes that he was not yet ready to trust me. I understood why; after all, he was still in shock from the change his life had recently taken.

Outside, Zephyr spent time in a smaller enclosure next the big wolf pack. In that location, people could observe him, but as time passed, Zephyr grew more disconnected to people and would stand off, away from visitors. At the same time, he let his guard down toward me and became my friend. After that happened, whenever I would enter his enclosure, Zephyr would run excitedly up to greet me, wagging his tail and licking my face. The young wolf was stunning and unusual looking, and he had a real defined look about him. I had never seen a wolf that looked quite as distinguished as Zephyr did.

Zephyr's fresh puppy face was very handsome, with strong features and black-tipped ears and tail, similar in looks to Nikkolah's soft tawny coloration. Zephyr had a coyote red-brown tint in his coat, which made him stand out with his own unique coloration. A jet-black lower lip seemed painted on like a clown. It looked like a permanent lipstick tattoo and sometimes gave a misleading appearance that Zephyr was smiling when in reality he was nervous. Zephyr was still very reserved around visitors, and he seemed most content to keep to himself. He was one of the shyest wolves I had known at that time and introduced me to the depth of the wolf's shy nature.

For companionship, Zephyr was introduced to Lucus's pack. At first, a fence separated the puppy and adults until all the wolves acclimated to one another. Then Zephyr was moved into the big wolf pack. Until then, though, the protective wire standing in between Zephyr and the wolves would allow them to investigate one another, and fingers crossed, no initial fighting would occur. If Cyndar's pack were to accept Zephyr, well, that seemed to be an ideal place for the little wolf to live. Zephyr could stay secluded on the rocky hill if he wanted, far enough away from human influence to live peacefully. When he was nearing nine months old, the gate between the pup and Lucus was opened, and in with Lucus, Cyndar, Nikkolah, Raven, and Jordan he eagerly went. In the beginning, it seemed Zephyr spent a lot of time following Lucus around and kissing up to him. The big wolf pen was large enough that the canines could get away from one another and spend time alone if they needed to, but Zephyr chose to frequent the attention of the older males.

As Zephyr grew into a yearling, he began to integrate himself into the pack hierarchy, and he quickly gained confidence and status. Zephyr found his place, working his way up the ladder of leadership. First he started with the girls, Raven and Jordan. His display of aggression toward them often seemed unnecessary, from my human eyes. Zephyr could be downright overbearing at times, and it made me realize how very insecure he must have been, living in the big wolf pack. Regardless if he already appeared strong from my view, what mattered to him was his social standing amongst his peers. As I watched these interactions happen, my mind always wanted to compare humans to wolves or vice versa. The way he was expressing himself toward the other pack members, especially the sisters, seemed cutthroat, and he was more aggressive than he was toward Lucus and Nikkolah. I believed Zephyr felt insignificant in his new family in order to behave with that much animosity.

In comparison to me, if I had acted out the way Zephyr did, and then lashed out at the others, it would have been embarrassing. I might recognize it was most likely due to my own lack of understanding or disrespecting their role. Or if it were as simple as searching for a place in the pack, then that kind of conduct could show a real lack of self-worth, at least in terms of human communications. Whatever reasons for Zephyr's behavior, excluding the aggression aspect, I could relate.

One day, Zephyr trotted over to greet me; as he went along, a breeze hit the top of the tree branches above him. The gentle wind lifted the branches up into the air and knocked a pinecone loose. The pinecone dropped silently and hit the ground next to him with a pop. From his reaction, he must have seen his life flash in front of his eyes. I teased Zephyr that he was a chicken disguised as a big wolf, running around shouting, "The sky is falling, the sky is falling!"

After a few months of living inside the big wolf pen, Zephyr grew tired of bullying Raven and Jordan. It was then he turned his focus to Nikkolah. As one may expect, Zephyr brought a far more intense attitude toward his peer. I could tell that he had a strong desire to be the alpha over Nikkolah from their first meeting. The little social climber became obsessed with elevating his rank over Nikkolah. And it may be that Nikkolah just gave in, getting tired of the constant testing and over-indulgent fighting that was involved with Zephyr. For whatever reason, in what felt like an overnight switch, Zephyr outranked Nikkolah and stood second to Lucus.

Nikkolah was second under Lucus by default, because up until the arrival of Zephyr, there was no other male wolf residing in the big wolf pack. Nikkolah appeared mostly subdued about Zephyr's whole takeover thing, and although he did his best to avoid Zephyr, it seemed his loyalty to Lucus would not bend. Nikkolah adored Lucus, and he would cower under the gentle yet firm leader, with complete admiration. Nikkolah's ever-wagging tail rapidly dusted the ground where Lucus stood. Nikkolah would pull his lips back tightly, exposing his perfect white teeth in a submissive gesture to the leader. Nikkolah wore this ear-to-ear grin in the presence of Lucus. It was moments like these that were a big threat to Zephyr. When Nikkolah was close to Lucus, all he could think about was Lucus. It did not matter to Nikkolah how many times in a day he got bullied by Zephyr.

In fact, it seemed that when Nikkolah was confronted by Zephyr, he became even more determined to remain at Lucus's side. When Nikkolah's display of submission to Lucus triggered Zephyr, he would pounce on Nikkolah like a lion in the hunt. The injuries were usually minimal. Nikkolah walked around with a face full of tiny bite holes, a living pincushion for Zephyr to stick his teeth into. Nikkolah would screech out toward Lucus as if to make sure Lucus saw that his faithful follower was under retaliation from the young Zephyr. It did not seem right to me, a younger wolf beating up on an elder; I asked myself whether this was like a human being. Before I could answer, a flood of memories and flashes of people who hurt their elders came pouring into my mind.

Nikkolah's pleas for rescue occasionally gained him attention. Lucus would run and charge Zephyr, growling intently but with a controlled confidence I wish Zephyr had. I hoped Lucus could set an example of how to lead with grace. Submitting, Zephyr would immediately take Nikkolah's place and begin to kiss up to Lucus, mirroring Nikkolah's body language down to the pulled tight lips. When Nikkolah was no threat or consequence to Zephyr, like when he was sleeping, this temporarily took the pressure off his social climbing. When Nikkolah was removed as competition, even if it was for only an hour nap, Zephyr seemed to relax. Animals from across the United States would come to call Mission: Wolf home, and it was difficult at best to predict which wolves would get along and who they would be happiest to stay with for life.

I wondered if there was an ancient, internal calling inside the psyche of wolves. Do wolves also bring forward imprints of ancestral beliefs? Driven by memories and opinions of parents and grandparents? The human mind carries forward many imprints from our relatives; some are positive, but many are negative, self-destructive thought patterns. The human mind holds on to disputes from times past, whether they are true or false; that programming is so strong that those thoughts become renewed personal truths for a new generation. These beliefs usually have little to no factual basis of comparison except "Grandpa said wolves are evil, ruthless killers." Was that how the mind of the wolf worked too? Or was it simply the need to be a leader?

What drive would make a wolf like Zephyr become aggressive in his actions toward the other wolves? Could it be genetics? Different subspecies of wolf put together by human hands into a pack situation would rarely—if ever—occur in the wild. Potentially this could add to the insecurity of his surroundings, like the falling pinecones and landing birds. For whatever reason, Zephyr seemed out of place in the big wolf pen. I liked it better when I saw him in the role of goofball solicitor, even if it was only temporary. It was a relief to see him flip upside down under Lucus and wag his tail, kissing up to his leader. Zephyr looked good playing and being carefree, even though it was all part of the game he was playing to seek social acceptance.

What I found interesting was wolves needed discipline from their alpha role models. That explained why Nikkolah frequently (and willingly) postured himself under Lucus. I remembered doing everything I could to avoid being reprimanded by my parents. This might be one way wolves understand their role in the pack and effect change. I could see the strain on Lucus from his two male pack mates competing to be his personal best; Nikkolah was content to keep Lucus as his leader, but by the way Zephyr acted, he seemed to have more in mind.

All things considered, as a captive pack of six intense wolves, Cyndar, Raven, Jordan, Lucus, Nikkolah, and Zephyr got through the summer season in one piece. Fall quickly turned into winter, and before we knew it, canine hormones began to take off. As their behavior began to exaggerate and skyrocket, we manually separated the male wolves from the females. Girls lived on one side of the big wolf pen, and the boys on the other. The day Cyndar, Raven, and Jordan went into heat, Lucus, Nikkolah, and Zephyr hit the fence running. Fast paced, back and forth they went, stopping long enough to look for any way they could find to get back in with the girls. For several stressful weeks, the males remained separated until the girls' hormones subsided, and they all began to return to normal behavior.

Once breeding season was over and done, a huge sigh of relief blanketed Mission: Wolf. It was difficult enough to manage the best care possible for the animals already living at the sanctuary without overpopulating the enclosures with puppies. In some ways, it would have been a blast having infant wolves around. But the reality of wolves in cages had taught us that at least a fifteen-year commitment was ahead. Resources would need to double, triple, or even more. Existing pens would need to expand; more help would be required to haul in the tons of food each week to feed all these hungry wolves. And most importantly, when the puppies grew up and changed into wild independent individuals, they needed to be with people who understood and were prepared to handle these changes.

We celebrated no wolf escapes and endured a few very minor injuries; Nikkolah had the most bite wounds to his nose, while Jordan had a fat lip from mouthing Raven, and that was it. We picked a quiet morning to open the gate and reunite the wolves. Excitement and high-energy enthusiasm filled the air as the wolves eagerly rushed the gates. The focus had now shifted. Instead of being infatuated with one another, they were interested in inspecting the opposite enclosures. It seemed a priority to remark their old scent posts. I laughed watching the wolves proceed with such urgency, running and completely ignoring one another until they had smelled the grounds and sufficiently refreshed their stamp of existence on their previous habitat.

Fresh territories, it seemed, were only fun and intriguing for the first few moments; then it was business as usual: find one another and re-establish their rank within the pack. Zephyr grew even larger in physical size and in his need to behave aggressively toward the others. Surprisingly, a couple of months after that separation, Zephyr again focused more aggression towards his female pack mates. There was a new resentment directed at Cyndar, which led to behaviors I had never seen before, nor did I expect to see. And I honestly wished I had never seen. It seemed common sense that younger members of the opposite sex in the wolf pack would have respect for their elder alpha opposites, as we do in the human world.

Unfortunately, another twist in the plot of Zephyr's world domination plan (aka the big wolf pen) unfolded when we saw that Zephyr had started ganging up with Raven in dominating Jordan. The two of them together would overwhelm Jordan and send her screaming and seeking shelter underground in a hole, inside a dugout, or under a dead tree. There, Jordan could tuck her butt inside the hole and defend her face until the two became bored and lost interest. At first, it seemed to go without saying that Cyndar was a tolerant leader that was immune to the advances of the juvenile social-climbing troublemakers. She easily stood her ground against Raven and Jordan, with little back talk from the sisters. Lucus and Nikkolah never seemed to consider challenging Cyndar for any reason. They might sneak away with her meat stash when she was not looking, but they were content with her as the alpha.

One morning, a young volunteer panicked after finding Cyndar beaten up and bloody, with multiple bite wounds on her body. At some point in the night into the early hours of the morning, it looked as if the younger wolves had ganged up on her. Although we were not certain exactly what happened, we speculated that she tried to stand her ground as best as she could. It was hard to believe just days before, Cyndar was the carefree leader of an intense wolf pack. Now she lay on the ground, near death. Once we realized the severity of her injuries, we immediately separated her away from the others. We hoped that she would heal from the wounds she had received and live a good long life.

There was a dense, undeniably dark energy present around Cyndar; it was as if she was depressed, and her heart had broken. She was suddenly an outcast, a far cry from the strong, proud, and humble leader she had once been. In my opinion, she was a refined and respectful leader, a fine example for any wolf to follow. My naïve human nature never expected that these wolves would go this far and injure her to this degree. Had Cyndar's pack been a free-roaming wild pack of wolves, and Cyndar a wild wolf, perhaps she could have gotten away. Could this be a curse of captivity? Unless she had some sickness or disease inside her that we did not know about, there was no good reason for this to happen.

With the exception of Zephyr, one very insecure and social climbing wolf who seemed to thrill at stirring up the alpha kettle with his aggressive actions. Where were Lucus and Nikkolah while all of this was going on? That was a question I never got an answer to. Mother's Day was just around the corner when I heard that Cyndar had died. It was a sad and shocking day; the day prior she seemed to perk up, and her eyes were sparkly, whereas before they had been hollow and empty. She seemed to smile when she saw Kent, as we approached her that final day. Thinking back on it, she knew that was the only way she could communicate with us, even though we did not understand at that time what her smile was saying.

Cyndar's loss was devastating for me, but it was especially hard on Kent. I could not imagine the wolves would feel any differently than we did. Kent bundled her fragile and delicate body up in a blanket, and we carried her out of the enclosure. As we left the gate and walked past the rest of the pack, we watched them to see if we could detect any signs of sadness or remorse. They stood there motionless and unconcerned as they watched us walk by; our own hearts quietly broken. To the people, Cyndar was a one-of-a-kind spirit; a role model of how any female should lead with grace and dignity. Although her life may have been short, in the time she did have, she lived a happy and powerful existence. She had been the first wolf to welcome me to Mission: Wolf.

Obviously, the big wolf pack knew more than we did. Perhaps she was sick with cancer or maybe it was something else entirely that caused the younger wolves to attack her so badly she died. Cyndar's death did nothing to end the brawling amongst the young wolves; rather, it spurred more warring between Raven and Jordan. Zephyr seemed to back off for a time and left the two sisters to figure out which one would be the new alpha female. For nearly six months on and off, vying back and forth, the squabbling continued. We considered separating them permanently, but at that time we were struggling just to keep the animals and ourselves alive. Besides, we would learn that bonded sisters would go to great lengths to be together.

Come to think about it, even if we had all the money in the world to buy miles of fence, and thousands of volunteers to put in months or even years of labor building on harsh rocky terrain, I believe the wolf pack would still be unhappy separated. The wolves would likely choose to stay together as a pack, even if the atmosphere appeared hostile to us. That seemed to be the way of the wolf, an animal that wanted desperately to live a pack life, even if that meant to the death.

CHAPTER 10

Woman Who Falls Behind Wolves

When the initial pain subsided, Shaman remained a ball of fury and protectiveness. He circled around me, watching Kent; his body was stiff and rigid.

Early one October morning, we drove to the beach on Montauk Island, located on Long Island, New York. Eager for a long run after being pent up inside the van for what seemed like a very busy week, presenting programs in front of thousands of people around the state. Kent opened his door first, hopped out, and hurried around to the back of the van. He unlatched the rear door and pulled out a box he kept stashed under Shaman's kennel. Inside was a special exercise leash made of finger-thin, thirty-foot-long steel cable. A carabiner was clipped to one end of the cable and a three-foot piece of steel chain attached at the other end to act as a collar around Shaman's neck. Excitement rose up in both canines, all the wiggling made it harder to get the collars clipped properly around their necks.

Shaman could barely contain himself, jumping from seat to seat, panting heavily as he did. A long lead would allow the animals to take more space away from the two-legged restrictions tethered behind. In a way, this would give the animals more freedom, but unfortunately, it also set us up for bigger potential falls if we made a mistake. As I left the van, I looked around and saw it was a

71

beautiful day. The clear blue sky cast a peaceful calm onto the water, and it looked like we could enjoy a run on a quiet beach. Littered with seashells and pebbles, the beach glimmered in the sun. Rocks smoothed over by years of beating to the tune of the saltwater waves. As I walked away from the van, not one other person was in sight; running with Shaman would be a good exercise.

Once we hit the sand, Shaman and I headed straight toward the water's edge. I found safety running closest to the water; the sand was smooth, and I did not sink, which allowed me to keep up with the wolf. I wanted to continue to run along the water's edge, but of course, Shaman and Lakoda wanted to move up higher to the rougher, rocky terrain. The smells and animal trails were more apparent there, at least according to the canines, whose priorities were to follow any animal trail they could find. The rocks on that part of the beach were misshapen, and the variety of sizes scattered across the ground made running very nerve racking.

I was trying to be mindful of how I ran, being aware that I did not land sideways on a rock or fall out of control. That meant I had to watch everywhere I stepped, keeping my eye on the ground. Shaman pulled harder as he took off running faster. The beach was an easy place for the canines to break into a full run and get their road-weary selves some release. And I wanted to release and relax into this run too, but I could not shake the feeling of anxiety bubbling up in my gut. I was still nervous I would fail walking Shaman on the leash, as I had back at the sanctuary. Shaman stopped ahead of me to investigate a smell where Lakoda had shown a brief interest. Lakoda was out ahead of Shaman, and I did not think much about that until Shaman did.

I gave a verbal "Slowdown" in hopes the wolf would hold up. My subconscious mind wanted to believe it was possible for me to communicate to the wolf with a thought or verbal word and get a response. Not this time, however; Shaman, concerned he was missing out on something, immediately ran to catch up with Lakoda. Of course, if Shaman were running on his own, he could catch Lakoda in a heartbeat. It was my concern that Lakoda and Kent were too far ahead to catch up to easily; clearly, that was not the wolf's concern. Even though the two were only ahead of us by several strides, running higher up on the shore.

As Shaman ran faster, with no sign of slowing down anytime soon, a red flag raised up in my mind. I should act before he hit rocket speed, a pace that did not match my eight-minute mile. I needed to slow him down before I was out of control and unable to. That likely would end my run, and I very much wanted to be successful running Shaman and stop on a positive note. I had made progress in many ways working with him, but I felt incomplete, simply due to my inability to exercise the wolf as I wished. In comparison, my two legs would not stand a chance next to Shaman's four; he had an obvious advantage over me.

Kent ran Shaman fast when he had him, so Shaman was used to running as he pleased, wild and in whatever direction he chose to go. Thanks to his background in skiing, Kent had enough stability and grace to maneuver over and around the rocks, sticks, and shrubs littering the ground. He somehow managed to keep up with Shaman and come out unscathed. Shaman wanted to pull on me like he did Kent, and that was at a different pace and freedom than I could manage. I felt like a puppet whipping around at the end of a string. The pace continued to near my limit. My strides became wider and wider as I tried my best to keep up with the powerful wolf.

I had no control over the direction we were running in whatsoever. Shaman could have easily pulled me into a blazing fire pit, and I could not have stopped it. Instead of fire, he headed into the rocks. He veered off into the thicker brush, running as if he were chasing a deer. I would not have believed his speed had I not felt it for myself; step after awkward step, I hung on to that leash for dear life. As Shaman flew forward at warp speed through the rocks and sticks, I was keenly aware that all my senses were pinging.

The sharp tang of the thick ocean air filled my nose, lungs, and head; the salty taste of sweat stained my lips. Exercise runs always sharpened my awareness to smells and other sensations as I ran through new and uncharted surroundings. I thought in part, too, and my senses were heightened because of the adrenaline rush I was experiencing, as I felt out of control, moving beyond my normal means. Feeling disconnected to my body, I worked hard to get enough strength to pull back the wrist and hand that connected me to this powerful canine. I wanted to steer Shaman away from the rocky terrain and back down toward the smooth sand before I was doomed to meet my maker. My legs were at their maximum capacity for motion, but that did not matter to Shaman, who continued toward the rocky terrain.

The allure of following animal trails into the grass seemed greater than any desire to run near the water. There, the sea would take any interesting and familiar smells Shaman recognized and understood and stripped those fragrances from the beach, replacing those smells with the scent of creatures Shaman had never encountered until that moment. Sea creatures like salty fish, shells, seals, and seagulls, animals of another world that, quite frankly, other than potential scent rolling in gull poop on the sand, Shaman had no intention of hanging around the waterfront. He was searching for familiar trails like the markings of strange dogs and wild deer.

I caught a quick break when he stopped to sniff a large seagull feather Lakoda was checking out. It was split and mangled by the elements of the sea and now lay plastered up against a rock. It looked as if it had weathered the waves a time or two. Shaman gently and delicately picked the feather up in his front teeth, and then, with a sharp little nip, the wolf severed it into pieces. Lakoda again took off, running ahead of Shaman. He looked like a giant bunny rabbit the way he hopped off with his fuzzy white butt bouncing up and down.

Lakoda was so excited to get to the grassy part of the beach and bury his nose in the smells of the local animals that he kept bounding farther away. Shaman continued to munch the feather, until he recognized how far away Kent and Lakoda had gotten. I enjoyed my brief moment of relief, watching for him to lose interest.

And in an instant, Shaman burst forward after Lakoda; as he darted faster, I knew he was rushing to see what Lakoda had found. Lakoda was digging and sniffing, engrossed in his discovery.

I could see the sand fly, and that seemed to excite Shaman all the more. Lakoda pulled out part of a dead fish from the sand and shook it out. He turned to run away when he saw Shaman rapidly approaching. Lakoda growled protectively of his new possession. Thinking he was protecting his prize, Lakoda now ran to get away from the curious wolf. Shaman, for the umpteenth time, forgot I was behind him and took off with such force he barely noticed the tug of me lingering behind him. If I believed my arms were short before this trip, all I had to do was run Shaman, and soon my arms would be dragging on the ground.

Shaman caught a whiff of dead fish; frantic to get face-to-face with the dog, he pulled me harder. I remember thinking I must have been taking those ten-foot strides each time my foot landed; again I felt like a little rag doll, flapping in the breeze behind Shaman. Kent was only a short distance ahead of us when Lakoda came to a stop in his tracks. He paused long enough to eat the fish before Shaman and I reached him. He better hurry, I thought as we reached the dog, working to choke down his find. Shaman circled curiously around Lakoda, looking and smelling to see what the malamute had. I tried to catch my breath and braced until the next time Shaman would bolt and then tow me behind him. As I stood panting while Lakoda tried to eat the fish, Kent saw his chance to reach down and take the fish away from Lakoda.

Kent tossed the fish in the opposite direction we were going, away from both animals. It took a few moments for Lakoda and Shaman to forget about the fish and focus on what was right in front of them. But once they did, we went back to running toward the beach, this time at a comfortable, reasonable speed. I wanted to run like this all the time; I was feeling much better and gaining my confidence until, without warning, we changed direction. Back up to the rocky part of the beach we went; both canines kicked up sand as they sped up.

Kent and Lakoda had gotten more than twenty paces out ahead of us, and I noticed how quickly I was again at a full run. This long-distance runner was being put to the test. I would have been a long-distance sprinter if I knew I was going to train to run with a wolf on a leash. We were nearly three miles away from the van, running at full speed. I was trying to keep up with two very fast, very strong canines and one very fast man. As I maneuvered my way through the rocks on the beach, I cannot remember exactly what happened next other than in a fleeting moment of distraction, I must have glanced away from where my feet were landing. In that split-second, I stepped on a rock the size of softball with my right foot, and the rock gave way. My ankle twisted hard underneath me, sending me straight to the ground. Pain shot up through my ankle into my leg. A shriek came out of my mouth, more in fear of my inability to take care of Shaman in that instant than from pain.

As I hit the ground on my side, the pain took over my mental capacity; all I could think about was my foot and leg. I worried I broke my ankle. I managed to hold tight on to Shaman, surprisingly with no problem. The big wolf circled around behind me, confused by my unusual behavior. Finally, Shaman was paying attention to me; unfortunately, when I was acting like a human freak show, rolling around on the ground and crying. After hearing all the commotion behind him, Kent stopped. Kent quickly turned Lakoda around and headed back towards us to help. It took us both by surprise when out of the blue, Shaman jumped up aggressively at Kent's approach. Shaman stood hackles up tail high, flapping his lips at Kent. "Baaahhh" reared its ugly head in the midst of me balling like a baby.

I almost laughed out loud through the tears. I think that may have been part of the problem. At the time, I was not aware that my reactions or responses to the wolf's protectiveness over me was actually rewarding the aggressive nature Shaman was displaying toward Kent. Shaman had been growing more and more testy with Kent as time passed and the wolf matured; come to think of it, most of the times I did laugh at these interactions. But in this instant, Shaman was growling his displeasure with much more intensity than his typical Baaahhh! And I was not laughing. This tone coming from his rolling jowls was much more grizzly bearish than I liked, not the sound we had grown accustomed to hearing. It was part of Shaman's nature to spar and vocally communicate with us. We would grow to expect and accept these outbursts. Whether the animal was eating raw meat or coming up for a greeting, there would be noises involved.

This was the first time that Shaman showed this level of protectiveness over me. Kent tried to ignore Shaman and continued to walk close to me; he wanted to take hold of Shaman's leash and help me, but with wolf teeth bared, Shaman used his whole body to block Kent.

Shaman's stiffening body language continued to grow as he puffed himself up like a peacock. His guard hair stood straight up, reaching out from the back of his neck, down through his lower back and to his tail. He wanted to make himself appear as tall as he possibly could on his four legs. If we listened to his body language, Shaman was making it very clear that Kent was not to come near me. And we did listen, because by the sounds coming out of his jaws, in this instant, Shaman seemed like a different animal. I felt helpless; after a few moments, the initial pain began to release, but I was afraid to stand on my foot. I sat there a few moments longer.

Kent had stopped just out of range of the angry wolf. I slowed my breathing down, trying to regain normal intake of air and stop sobbing. I decided to stay still at least until the ankle stopped throbbing, and I calmed down. As the initial pain began to subside, Shaman remained a ball of fury and protectiveness. His upper body remained rigid while his legs moved deliberately, taking short, intentional steps, circling in between the two of us. He did not take his eyes off of Kent. He was so focused on keeping Kent away from me that it seemed as if he blamed Kent for what had happened.

Or if I looked at it as Shaman might see what was happening, I might believe that by seeing my weakness, Kent would want to take advantage and finish me off. What else would go through the mind of a wolf? The irony was that a large black wolf now guarded me and was keeping away the one person whose help I needed the most. I looked up at Kent through my tears, and he looked helplessly back at me.

"You're going to have to walk him yourself," he said, discouraged.

There was nothing Kent could do to help me, because Shaman would not let him. After sitting on the ground for about ten minutes, I stood up on my left leg and hesitantly tried to put weight on my right leg. It hurt like crazy, and there was little I could do about it but deal with my situation. I focused on what was in front of me, got up, and began to limp back toward the van.

When I remembered that we were nearly three miles away from the van, I almost started to cry again. I could see that Kent was disappointed, not only because he was helpless, but also because of Shaman's actions toward him. If I were Kent, I would be devastated and feel like I lost a precious animal friend I had raised. I had to focus on the present and gather together the long lead. I had to be fully responsible for this very strong male wolf that I could barely handle with two good legs and that now believed Kent was somehow a threat. Kent walked near me and did so slowly, keeping Lakoda at a walk. Shaman watched him like a hawk and walked in between the two of us, all puffed up and territorial.

That run was one of the most difficult times that I had experienced handling wolves. Walking that far with an injured leg, it was all I could do to hold on to Shaman. Kent and Lakoda walked near me, and Shaman remained preoccupied with where they were at all times. The big wolf did not pay much attention to me hobbling along behind him. He just continued to pull on the lead. That walk back seemed to take hours. When the four of us finally reached the van, Kent walked out ahead of me and opened the sliding door. Shaman jumped up and returned safely back to his kennel and to non-threatened state of mind. For the rest of that trip, I hobbled around and could not walk either Shaman or Lakoda that was probably for the best. I will always remember that day as the ultimate eye-opener, beyond being pulled into a tree or knocked down the hill back at MW.

We continued on the journey despite the fact that I had sprained my ankle and was limping. The show must go on, and we had a schedule to follow, and many people were excited to see Shaman. I felt pretty useless and did what I could to be helpful. Kent handled Shaman, but Shaman's attitude toward Kent had changed in my presence. He continued his short-tempered attitude with Kent when I was near, but as long as I did not get in between the two, Kent could work with Shaman. It appeared I was traveling with two boyfriends, one of them was more jealous than any boyfriend I ever had.

The next stop was Chicago, where we would present Shaman to several schools in the city. Many schoolchildren were excited to learn about wolves this visit.

One stop at a gas station, Kent drove the van up to the first available gas pump, stopped the engine, climbed out, and shut the door behind him. While he was outside, he decided to get two racks of beef ribs from the cooler under Shaman's kennel. Shaman heard what Kent was doing and immediately knew what was happening and got excited. Kent quickly opened the door and tossed in the rib racks; with big eager canine teeth, both Shaman and Lakoda grabbed their rack without hesitation. They growled and fussed at one another as they went about deciding who would get which rack. Lakoda was being outranked on many things, especially food, then rushing to claim a private space in the van to eat without the influence of the other.

I got up out of my seat and moved over to the driver's seat for a moment to stretch and sit differently for a few moments while Kent filled the tank. As I sat back and looked out the window, I enjoyed a moment of stillness. I thought my timing was good as Shaman had turned and ran to the safety of his kennel. There he could guard his ribs against Lakoda. "Rip! Smack! Bang!" Shaman slammed his rack of ribs down on the wooden floor as he tore into the meat between the bones.

"You sure make a lot of racket and a big production out of eating rib bones," I said out loud to Shaman. I did not see Lakoda when he decided he was going to crowd in with Shaman inside the kennel and moved in right behind the wolf. I had half started to daydream when Shaman unexpectedly launched himself face and raw meat rack first into my lap, landing right on top of my thighs. Vulnerability shot up in my body as the big wolf proceeded to dig in and start eating again on top of my legs. What the heck happened? I turned just enough to see that Lakoda had taken over Shaman's place in the kennel.

Somewhat shocked and definitely caught off-guard, I started to sit up and then realized my face was near his rack of ribs. I leaned back and tried not to look at Shaman. Lakoda's intrusion on Shaman's space catapulted the wolf forward, up into my lap. I did not know why Shaman decided to get on top of me; there was plenty other free space in the van. Reluctantly, I went with it and froze because Shaman had such a sensitive, highly volatile food drive. I could feel in my legs the noise from the meat being torn off the thick beef rib bones. Fear of being bitten or pinched unintentionally if Shaman missed the rib rack crossed my mind; I could not help it, nor did I dare move. With ferocity unique to Shaman, he pulled the meat from the bones with quick, precise grabs. Like a calculated machine, Shaman was graceful in his moments of ugly, and it came as naturally to him as if he were trotting peacefully across a meadow.

Breathing heavily, his nose pushed the rib bones down again into my leg, holding them so delicately with his huge paws. The motion of his jaws locking on the meat and tearing it upward must have made my whole body move. I had a whole new appreciation for the term "wolf it down." Minutes passed by, and Shaman was about done eating his rack of ribs. Kent had finished filling the gas tank, walked back around to the passenger side door, and flung it open. This sudden motion again made Shaman fear for the possession of his rack of ribs. Carrying the ribs in his jaws, Shaman retreated back to the bench in front of the kennel where Lakoda lay, still enjoying his bone peacefully. Kent was surprised as to what he saw when he opened the door, and I brushed off my pant legs. A bloody, oily substance was smashed into the fabric of my jeans. I knew that was something I would never forget.

CHAPTER 11

Wolf Pup Needs a Home

As I focused on frantically digging, Sila instantly lost interest in the fox; after all, what I was doing briefly appeared more exciting.

In the summer of 1990, a vivacious little creature named Sila came to us; ironically, she was Rowdy's half-sister, and like him, she was sold as a pet from the same roadside zoo. We believed that her and Rowdy's mother had Arctic ancestry. Sila was much younger than Rowdy; at a few months old, we could work with her easier. She had developed a reputation as a little terror and had been causing all kinds of trouble for her previous human family. The owner of the wolf pup had asked a friend for advice on the pup's difficult behaviors and she recommended the family bring the little terror to Mission: Wolf.

The owner believed he had made a smart decision getting a wolf as a pet, after investing a lot of time in reading as many different books that he could find. He was very upset to learn that after all the expense, preparation, and hard work he went through to bring home a wolf pup, she was much more than he could handle. And to top it off, his family had really taken a liking to the little terror. The last straw occurred the day the little pup ran out the door and took off down the street to a neighbor's house. Making her little body right at home, she ran inside an open door and proceeded to steal a loaf of bread off the counter top. The neighbor was home at the time and was surprised to see a little wild thing run in the door off the street.

Sila challenged the neighbor, growling at him as he tried to protect his property and get the loaf of bread back. Not long after that incident, Sila came to Mission: Wolf. The family had named the wolf pup "Sila" after an Eskimo word meaning "of all things" or "all creation." When Sila first arrived, I thought she looked like a little piglet; maybe it was her energy around food that overtook her personality and turned her into a beast. She was the second youngest pup I had been around and the first wolf pup to hand raise.

Up to that point, I had not seen many wolf pups. It seemed impossible to know if Sila was a pure wolf, so we took her at face value. She looked and acted like a wolf, therefore she would be treated like one. Sila was young enough we thought she might work in well with Shaman, Bear, Ghost, Navarre, and the others at the sanctuary, and we hoped she would do well on the road with Shaman and Lakoda in the Ambassador wolf program. She was outgoing enough around new people, and that might become a welcome addition to the Ambassador program. Her strong-headed and belligerent behavior made it immediately clear why her previous owner had problems with her. She had no manners around food and became as fierce as a full-grown grizzly bear when eating was involved.

Sila had a different side to her personality; when she was not threatened, she was charming and appealing in a funny way. It was distressing to see her intensity around food; she became as protective and stressed as any full-grown wolf, but in a small, undeveloped body. We decided that anytime she had food or bones, we would leave her alone and not confront her in any way, at least as best as we could. To put Sila into Shaman's enclosure was a good thing. She immediately thought he was really something. She adored Shaman and loved nothing better than to follow him around and be part of his every move. Shaman liked to be left alone and acted independent and aloof around her.

Because of Shaman's distance, Sila often seemed insecure around him. This insecurity instigated small dominance brawls or spats between the two. Sila and Shaman had a funny relationship. Sila really rallied him up when she solicited attention from him, and the more she did, the more fired up he became to boss her around. Shaman would get intense with Sila, using his mouth, teeth, and vocal abilities. He was our best way of dealing with Sila's food issues. He had a clear-cut plan around food, and it was straightforward and simple.

No food was off-limits to Shaman. He acted like all food belonged to him and only him, no questions asked. Bear, a wolf dog cross however, did not agree with the big wolf's food hoarding. And from a distance, she would lift her head up toward him and let out a loud warning growl if he even looked at her meat. She was not convinced that Shaman was sole owner of all the food. Regardless, without hesitation, Bear ate up her food before Shaman could prove otherwise. It was not long before Shaman made the rounds in the enclosure, searching for loose pieces of meat. He often stole any meat that was not in his possession and made it his. Shaman took away any food Sila did not eat up right away, sometimes pulling it right out of her mouth.

Sila herself shared the same food-hoarding trait as Shaman, and the first couple of times Shaman took her meat, she protested and tried to win it back. Nothing she could do would challenge Shaman; he won the round every time. Shaman displayed no sympathy toward the new punk pup, either. He was like a rough-and-tumble older brother that gave his sister tough love. Sila was resilient and quickly recovered and moved on, making her way around the grounds in search of any other food scraps that may have been dropped by the other canines. Being as strong willed as Shaman in her own right, she did not let the big wolf's reluctance toward her hold her back; she continued to test her limits with him.

As a test, we took a short van trip to Boulder with young Sila and Shaman. We could see how much Sila's presence in the Ambassador wolf program could really help Shaman be more at ease in the public. Sila took to the role of Ambassador wolf as if she were born to do the job, often to our pleasant surprise. She was the exact opposite of Shaman in many ways: brave and outgoing with people, unlike Shaman, who had grown into quite an independent creature. Back at the sanctuary, Shaman and Sila behaved differently toward one another. General daily living inside the enclosure was comical to watch; the dynamics between Shaman and his new apprentice, Sila, were charged with his short temper. Shaman was often annoyed by Sila to the core and would lash out at her.

Shaman constantly disciplined Sila for anything; just her presence was enough to set him off. All she had to do was look in his direction, for any reason, and he'd respond with "Baaahhh!" In spite of this, Sila adored Shaman and constantly asked for more. Mouth open, Shaman would grab her by the head with his teeth and she would squeak like a little toy. Shaman was a secret weapon to get through to the little pig-headed Sila. Both wolves had strengths they unwittingly used to help each other, and their weaknesses and insecurities that would lead them to squabble, much in the very same ways people do. Shaman would be a good teacher or mentor for Sila in many ways; it was heart-warming to watch the two together.

Shortly before we left for a big Ambassador wolf tour to the East Coast, where we would be gone for months, we were given an antelope that had been hit by a car. One day, a man showed up in the driveway with this antelope carcass; it was a road kill he had picked up, and he was very excited and proud to bring it to feed the wolves. The problem we faced at the time was, one small antelope would not feed all the wolves at the sanctuary. That meant we had to cut it up and disperse it as best we could, adding other meat so everyone was fed. Sila and Shaman were temporarily sharing one of the larger enclosures with wolf dog crosses Navarre, Crimzon, Haida, Ghost, and Dancing Bear. At the time, they were all one big happy group of youngsters. But during feeding time, it was a different story; dinnertime for the pack of misfits often resembled a shark feeding frenzy. There was a hierarchy, even though many times it did not appear that way.

Navarre was the biggest and burliest of the group, and of course he was the big-time king wolf dog over Shaman and over Lakoda. Lakoda did not spend much time in the pack; instead, he had been taken out and retired to full-time housedog. That meant Navarre was Shaman's new acting superior, at least for the time being, until we took Shaman and Sila on the fall tour. Navarre was a bully to his pack, including his sister Crimzon. Navarre also tried to bully people; occasionally, he would even hike his leg and mark someone. He was a real tough cookie with an unusual quirk. When we took Shaman and Sila out of the enclosure, be it for one hour or a week, it was a real hoot to watch Navarre reunite with them.

As soon as Navarre saw the van turn into the parking lot, he would run to the gate entrance and begin jumping up and down, as if he were on a trampoline (he repeated the same behavior whenever the meat truck came and went). It only worked to take Shaman and Sila out of Navarre's pack for a short time. And it worked out that Navarre was alpha everything, but he could not outdo Shaman during feeding time. Shaman was too quick and moved faster than Navarre could even think to move. Which left Navarre at somewhat of a disadvantage during mealtimes.

We cut up the antelope and added enough beef to make a large feeding for Navarre and Shaman's pack. Carrying the meat in buckets, we charged into the enclosure with the animals, holding the buckets out in front of our bodies as hungry canines mobbed us. Navarre typically charged right in first and claimed the largest piece of meat for himself, and this time was no different. He grabbed the antelope's head out of Kent's bucket and took off running down the hill with it in his mouth. However, that did not last long. With all the animals in the enclosure, each one running in a different direction, confusion abounded. And suddenly, Shaman was running up the hill with the antelope head in his mouth. He went a short distance and then stopped and began eating.

Sila and Bear had each gotten a front leg of the antelope and ran off down the hill, away from Shaman, to eat. Bear found a place where she felt safe, and both canines lay down right next to one another to eat. Sila mirrored Bear, watching her eat her antelope leg. Bear was busy eating, yet that did not stop her slobber filled, sharp warnings directed at Sila. Sila would snap right back. After Sila had eaten what she could on the leg, Navarre came and stole it, and after she had eaten all she could find, she focused her attention on Shaman and the antelope head. I happened to be in the pen at the time with my camera, and took a photo of Shaman guarding his prize from the other canines, that is the image at the end of chapter 8.

Shaman growled, Baaahhh-ed, and spit at Sila, who relentlessly spent a good part of that day dancing around him and begging, to no avail. Later, we left with Shaman and Sila together in the van for the first time, and thankfully, Sila was a natural when it came to traveling in the wolf van. We learned to work with her belligerent personality in complementary ways for all involved (at least most of the time).

During exercise runs, we put Shaman and Sila on thirty-foot steel cables. The point was to let the wolves run as fast as they could with the freedom to go wherever they wanted to go. It was their time to be themselves, to get a break from the traveling, from the van, and with a distance of thirty feet, a break from us too. I regard Sila as my first real wolf teacher when it came to using the leash as a form of communication and dance, rather than being constantly pulled around behind. I believed that because Sila had a lot of free running time as a pup, she had very little desire to be leashed. She became really bull headed when I put her on the leash. But there was a place that I could reach her; however hard she would pull, if I held pressure at the right moment, she would give in and stop pulling.

Unknown to me at that time, this dance with Sila would go on for years. Often during runs, the only reminder that she would feel of me behind her would be a stop if she ran out too far ahead or went faster than I could keep up with. She was much easier to handle on a leash than Shaman was. Of course, she was much smaller. Sila was more responsive on the leash, again probably due in part to the work of her previous owner, who started her on a leash at a young age. Still, there was a strong-willed side to Sila; if she wanted to go somewhere, ultimately, she would try.

This first tour east was a particularly long trip; Shaman had relaxed his judgment of Kent, now that I exercised Sila almost exclusively and, for the most part, everything went pretty well. I felt much more confident behind the leash of Sila, as if I were more of a match, except when she got wet. If she got wet, especially when it was cold, she became so fired up she would race circles around me, and then she'd run wide-eyed at Kent and Shaman. I learned a good exercise early on with Sila that helped me tremendously, and that was to ground myself like an ancient oak tree. This exercise introduced me to using my body in an energetic way; opening a door that as time passed would broaden my understanding of different ways energy works with animals. I really loved to do meditation and eventually created my own version. I believe there are as many different versions of this kind of grounding meditation as there are unique souls doing them.

As I would begin to visualize myself becoming a tree, a powerful, connected feeling would rise up inside of me. I assumed, at first, this was because of my love of trees. In my mind's eye, I would see huge tree roots come out from under me and grow down to the center of the earth. I would visualize colors as I went along too. It was important to see the roots strong and tightly connected to the earth, a connection so strong that I could not be moved from the ground I stood on, no matter what. So each time I reminded myself that I needed to be extra strong and confident handling Sila, I would do a quick visualization, and re-ground myself so to speak, and reconnect my energy to the planet.

Visualization would become a standard part of my experience when traveling with the wolves and beyond. Once I learned how amazingly it really worked with Sila, I wished I had known about it sooner to use it with Shaman or Nikkolah. It also really opened my eyes to the world of energetic work and the potential to harness a deeper level of self-control and understanding that connected what I truly believed about my own intuition.

Sila was growing into a very tall wolf; at times, her size was intimidating to people. Shaman was often intimidating to people based on his size too, but for him, it was more about the way he looked. His yellow eyes stood out from his black fur as if they were lit up from behind. The personality difference between the two canines was like day and night. Sila took any intimidation that was presented her and turned it to love. Her brave, bull-headed energy blasted right past any person's wall of fear, ultimately teaching them she was not to be feared. Aloof Shaman, on the other hand, was a crystal-clear mirror.

Shaman reflected any intimidation he received from people right back to them. People who were fearful of Shaman, he would generally stay away from or ignore. Sila seemed to have no hang-ups or fears about anyone; to judge any person was not in her understanding. She made almost everyone she met smile and feel comfortable around her. Sila eagerly greeted everyone with love and enthusiasm, even if they were intimidated by her big white wolfiness. And she often got people over their fear of her just being who she was.

It was during this time I really began paying attention and learned how important it was for the wolves to use their noses. Everywhere we went, whether we were out for exercise or inside a building for programs, Shaman and Sila were ever ready to investigate new smells. During these outings, I saw them use their noses for different reasons. Shaman, the more timid wolf, used his nose to break the ice; in what appeared to be a good way for him to accept meeting new people, he would smell his way up to them. That is basically what he did that very first day I met him back at the university campus. He used his nose like feelers around the room. On the other hand, he also used his nose as an excuse to leave any place he felt uncomfortable. Sometimes an occasional smell would become so intoxicating to Shaman, he appeared lost in it, not paying attention to anything else.

One of the stops that fall was in Quechee, Vermont. We didn't know it when we first arrived, but the Nature Center there was one of the most "scent-o-licious" places for the wolves to be. Especially Sila. We arrived at the Vermont Institute of Natural Science (VINS) for an evening of programs. The wolves were eager to get out of the van after traveling all day across the state. We were running behind and had a lot of driving to do. Shaman and Sila had to sit tight a bit longer while Kent and I hurried to set up the tables and Kent prepared his talk.

As we walked around the room and set up chairs for the guests, we noticed the room was filled with different taxidermy animals. The room was small, and the wolves always drew a large crowd; with those dead animal smells in there, it was going to be difficult to keep the wolves calm. The center was very understanding and accommodating around the concern to bring the wolves in to the space with the dead critters visible.

"Most of these furries could be stored away," the director told us, in so many words.

We stashed them in the white cabinets that lined the wall at the back of the room, along the floor. There, the animals should be safe from the wolves. Some of the animals and birds had already been placed high up on shelves almost to the ceiling.

The white cabinets doors could be pulled open; they had magnet stays on them. At the time, I did not think it was of any consequence (out of sight out of mind) and did not really pay much attention. There were bird displays as well as several critters, including a good-sized fox that I picked up and stashed inside one of the cabinets. I remember setting it down on one of the lower shelves and pushing it against the back as far as I could reach. We moved the chairs around in a horseshoe manner, in the best way we could so the audience could see. We would use the space in the center of the room for the wolves to be in.

People arrived early to see the program, and Kent was getting ready to start. He gave a short talk before we brought in the wolves. He warned the audience to stay calm and quiet and remain in their seats when the wolves were in the room. It is not an easy job to manage people in a small atmosphere, and then add in a sensitive animal like a wolf to the middle. Not to mention any last-minute people wandering in late to the program. Kent would bring them all up to speed, so everyone knew how to behave when the wolves were in the room. While he continued to talk to the audience, I brought the wolves in one at a time.

Shaman came bounding out of the van with excitement; his energy was still reeling from being cooped up after the long drive. He had been to the VINS center before and remembered the smells of the parking lot; being a nature center, there were lots of attractive smells to explore, and I could feel his energy level come up. He, in his mind, was ready to take off in an exercise run, not stand indoors in a small venue, all calm and patient. He's full of energy; *more energy than the room could hold*, I thought. Shaman blasted through the door ahead of me with a huff; I felt like I had a brief work out, short but powerful. I handed Shaman's leash to Kent and went right back out to get Sila. Having been left alone for two minutes, Sila had worked herself up into a frenzy of excitement, making it nearly impossible for me to get a hold of her and put the collar around her neck.

She would not stand still and kept reeling around me like a spinning top, almost making me dizzy, and then jumping up and looking out the window for Shaman.

"If you would just stand still, Sila, I could get your collar on and we could go," I would tell her; once I finally got a hold of her and opened the van door, she mirrored Shaman's enthusiasm, only with a little more pull, as if she were feeling left out. Sila jumped out of the van and pulled me across the parking lot to the entry door. I held the door open so she did not catch her toes in it as she rushed through. I waited until she cleared the door and then pulled the door shut behind us.

The audience and the staff of the Nature Center all looked at Sila with anticipation. Sila immediately ran up to Shaman. "I missed you!" "You left me!" As she briefly expressed her concern momentarily reestablishing her place with Shaman as she mouthed him repeatedly. Once she settled down enough to walk around a little, the people in the front row distracted Sila. I can't remember if anyone got much of a greeting, because she was caught up in her nose. She wanted to smell their pant legs and shoes and that was it.

I was busy watching both wolves; the unsettled high energy they exuded was a bit nerve racking for me. I worked to get both of them to slow down, by trying to distract them and bring their attention to the center of the room, but Sila would have none of it. I was certain they had caught on to the smells of all the dead animals around the room. Sila impatiently walked back and forth in the small room, pulling harder on her leash than normal. Shaman was more restricted, due to the fact that Kent was talking to the audience and standing in the center of the room. Sila pushed the limits of the invisible fence perimeter I had set up in my mind for her to stay behind. She wanted to walk closer to the audience.

With her nose to the floor, she became so caught up with smells that she did not know which direction to go first. Unsure where the best smells were coming from, she tried to decide for herself. I was sure if we let her loose in the room, she probably would be jumping around, heading in different directions all at once, until she found the right trail to follow. All the taxidermy animals lay safely tucked away, hidden in other rooms or inside the sturdy cabinets. Even though we wanted Sila to focus on the audience and Shaman, those stuffed animals and birds had been there for many years, and the smells had permeated the room. To the wolves, the smells were irresistible.

It was a challenge for us to keep the animals in the center of the room, where everyone could see. Shaman and Sila were full of energy, and it took several moments to settle down. I felt like the taxidermy animals were safe, "out of sight, out of mind," right?

To my dismay, Sila caught wind of the cabinet where I had stashed the fox. I had hoped to avoid that whole side of the room if possible. The problem was, that was part of the open free space the wolves had to investigate during the program. It was challenging enough to keep their high energy contained in such a small space, but then add in the smells of long-dead animals. Sila belligerently pulled me in the direction of the cabinet doors, stopping a few doors down from the fox. I let her step out ahead of me, believing the cabinet doors were shut tight enough that Sila would smell the outside of the door and move on. The audience watched quietly as both wolves wandered around, exploring the room and listening to Kent talk about the wolves.

Sila slowly made her way down the row of the cabinets, intently sniffing the outside of each door inch by inch, one by one. She then moved away to a smell a table located a few feet in front of the cabinet door where the fox was. As she moved away from the cabinets, I took a moment to look over at Shaman. He was in the same mode as Sila, his nose to the ground, sniffing the floor and chairs by the audience. Sila reached her head up to the tabletop, twisting her nose sideways as she stretched, sniffing the surface that most likely held countless smells. As Kent continued his talk, I realized that the wolves had finally settled down. I relaxed and breathed a sigh of relief.

I paused to gather up the short length of chain hanging down Sila's neck to the floor. I was excited about what I was learning, using the leash as more than just a chain hooked to her neck. Finding a new connection to Sila was one of the best things I had done so far. I had enough experience being jerked around at that point to see the value of testing pressure release as a tool for communication and direction. Sila seemed to respond well if I varied the amount of tension I held on her neck and did not constantly hold her in a pressured headlock. As I turned my body to face the audience, Sila decided to turn back around toward the cabinets again. She hesitated briefly in front of the door, as if she were trying to get my attention away from the cabinets. In the blink of an eye and one quick turn, Sila went for the right cabinet and came out with the fox in her mouth.

It was as if she knew exactly where to go, like she energetically traced the path my hand created earlier, reaching in to stash the fox. Or was it her powerful sense of smell? Perhaps it went even deeper into a connection I had yet to understand. What if Sila could read my mind? Regardless, it did not matter how Sila got the door open so fast; she knew exactly where to find it. Before I could move, she dove under the shelf and emerged with the fox in her mouth. She "outfoxed" me.

The fox was out of the bag (pun intended). I was blown away at the speed Sila got the fox, and what I was seeing happen right in front of me, and in a flash, a protective predator came out in Sila. She was elevated to a new level of nasty with her newfound possession. She roared a deep, guttural, ferocious growl toward Shaman, warning him to stay back. Kent looked at me with a puzzled look on his face as if to ask what I was going to do about it. I knew immediately that Sila was not going to let me have the fox.

Sila's snarling lips wrapped tightly around the fox carcass. She had grabbed the attention of every audience member and gotten Shaman very excited. Kent had to work to keep Shaman back away from Sila and the fox. If he had made it over to the scene, it would have exploded beyond anything I cared to experience (or clean up, for that matter). Kent at the same time was also trying to narrate what was happening to the audience, explaining the posturing and intense behavior Sila was displaying over the fox toward Shaman. I also saw the problem it was causing Kent, who was trying to deal, in the most graceful way he could, with Shaman, who was focused on the fox.

I knew I did not want to get myself bitten by Sila over a stupid dead fox, but I had to act quickly and do something. I was unsure exactly what to do, and in a snap decision, I put pressure on Sila's leash; she reluctantly followed behind me, with fox in mouth, right out the back door. Once outside, I had to quickly decide how I was going to get the fox away from Sila and out of sight from Shaman, who was watching us through the large glass window. With a tight grip on Sila's chain, I walked her into the parking lot. I hovered down over her head, and she continued to be protective, but not with the intensity she had inside. She had lightened up some, feeling the fox was all hers without the threat of Shaman's presence.

As we moved into the parking lot, I saw a stick lying on the ground in front of me. Sila was in the mode to stop and get down to business, tearing the fox apart. I did not want to ruin the center's display, so I reached down and grabbed the stick. Sila roared at me in her possessive, guttural roar, thinking I was going for the fox. I bent down and leaned away from Sila, toward the stick. I quickly took the stick with my free hand and, with purposeful movements, began to dig in the dirt off to the side, away from where Sila was mouthing the fox.

As I did this frantic focused digging, Sila instantly lost interest in the fox; after all, what I was doing seemed more exciting. She dropped the fox on the ground next to me. I tossed the stick a few feet ahead of where the fox now rested in the dirt. Sila jumped forward again with a competitive whim, wanting to get the stick before I could. While she went after the stick, without hesitation, I reached down and grabbed the fox in my hand. As I did so, I realized there was no place for me to put the fox once I had it. Nowhere was far enough out of reach of Sila. Once she figured out what I had just done, she would try to grab the fox from me, maybe even biting me in the process.

I grabbed hold of the fox with distressed energy that had come up in me; I felt prompted to act without really thinking. I called forward my automatic rapid-fire reflexes and threw that fox upward with all my might. "Pop!" The fox hit the roof. I must have turned red in embarrassment at that moment, and I looked around to see it anyone from the audience was watching. I realized how silly it must look to an unsuspecting onlooker. Once the fox was out of Sila's sight, though, it was out of her mind.

I took a deep breath and gathered up Sila's lead, turning her back toward the door. She looked up at where the fox had landed on the roof of the Nature Center and briefly lifted her head up to sniff.

"Good-bye, fox!" I said to myself, relieved. I was embarrassed to show my face and wished I could just vanish or pretend it did not happen. We began to walk back into the room, calmly, until Sila saw Shaman.

Then the reuniting between the two canines commenced. Shaman was confused and a little pent up after watching all the excitement of the fox; he had wanted that fox, it was clear. He had to tell Sila about it, too, through biting down on her nose and making her drop to the floor and squeal in submission. There was laughter in the room as the two tried to drown out the laughing. Kent laughed and said that they had seen us disappear out the door, and then they had heard a roar and a thump.

I explained what I did when we went outside: "I distracted Sila by digging in the dirt of the parking lot with a stick. When Sila lost interest in the fox and dropped it long enough for me to get hold of it, my guttural reaction was to throw it up on the roof. I did not know what else to do with it."

Everyone laughed. If we had allowed Sila to keep the fox, it would have caused a big fuss with Shaman. Not to mention she would have definitely shredded the fox into pieces and maybe even scent rolled on it (or peed on it). Sila behaved worst when she was being possessive. She was a great teacher of the intensity and seriousness wolves put into possession of food or a material object.

To Sila, it did not matter; when she got it in her head that she wanted something, I could not take it away without a loud outburst. We learned early in our relationships with the wolves that the power of distraction to avoid conflict over possessions of material objects was the most effective way to handle any potential problem. Food, on the other hand, was a whole different story. We had no control over food-possessive behaviors, and unless it was something that might cause harm, we did not engage. Distraction would become a life-long friend in my dealings with these wild, possessive-minded canines.

Sila was an amazing teacher of many life lessons beyond possession to me. One of the most important lessons I would learn working with her was not to be so unconscious or insensitive during my walks. When I walked Shaman, I had to hold on for dear life; all he did was pull, pull, and pull on the leash. Therefore, I never gave any consideration to pulling back hard on him. Sila, however, reacted much differently, looking up at me when I pulled hard, as if I were hurting her, causing her to cough or get choked up if I held on. She taught me to think about the pressure I was putting on her neck with the leash.

Sila had a soft side that she exposed to me during our walks. This soft side taught me to become more sensitive to how much pressure I put on her neck. It was true that the previous experiences I had with Shaman and Nikkolah had toughened me up, but this was different. For the first time, I had an insight that I could use the leash as a communication tool and not just a control tool. From that moment on, I decided to try letting up on the pressure I put on her neck during our walk. Like the beginning of a dance, if Sila jumped forward and pulled pressure on me, I in turn held pressure on her. Once she let up, I too let up and released pressure.

The simple act of paying attention to the connection I had to Sila's led was the start of something real and special. What a great way to change a stressful walk into a fun and fluid dance, true to my artist's nature. During that time, I put into action the oak tree meditation. It took a few tries for me to understand how this meditation worked but when I did get it, and I could visualize my roots deep in the ground, to my surprise I found it really worked. I became grounded to the earth like never before. Oak tree meditation helped me become stronger on my feet; I was not knocked around as easily.

Anytime I knew I needed a little extra strength when handling Shaman or Sila, I would do a quick visualization and reground my roots. It became a standard practice for me during my walks with the wolves, and it made my heart sing. Working freely and naturally with the wolves was how I wanted all my relationships with them to be. It went against my very nature to force the animals into anything. This one small change to my thought process opened a whole new world of energy and visualization to help animals. It inspired me to seek out more meditation, more visualization, and more energy work. I wanted to find as many ways as I could to practice using my intuition and visualization on both myself, and the canines in my life.

Sila pulls Tracy downhill. Photograph courtesy Gary Crandall.

CHAPTER 12

Terrible Threes

No matter where we were, or whom we were in front of, Shaman felt no inhibitions to show us exactly what he was feeling toward Kent.

Everything changed when Shaman turned three. During his third year, it became increasingly more difficult for Kent to handle him, both at the sanctuary and in public programs. Shaman very much perceived Kent as part of his pack; unfortunately, he looked down on Kent. Shaman was alpha of the relationship, and there was no changing the wolf's thought process. In a way, Kent predicted it during his talks with people regarding the life span of wolves kept as pets. During the presentations, Kent's focus was overshadowed by the presence of a large black wolf giving him the eye. Not an evil eye, mind you; rather, a disciplinary eye.

Kent's behavior toward Shaman had to be exactly right from the wolf's perspective, or Shaman would get his feathers ruffled. Let me rephrase that into wolf terms: get his hackles up and go "Baaahhh!" It seemed that "Baaahhh" was the word of the day every day, and often all day long, any reaction Shaman had toward Kent was the same. To say the least, Kent was beginning to lose confidence in his relationship with Shaman.

I had been traveling through the States with Kent and Shaman, on and off, for the better part of two years. I mostly handled Lakoda and Sila in the programs, but my time was increasingly being spent with the intense big wolf. Kent had developed into a very captivating and inspiring speaker. Hundreds of people filled the venues to hear him speak about wolves, which he was very passionate about. I also began to recognize just how challenging public speaking was. During the wolf presentation, Kent gave his full attention to the audience, and it paid off. He knew instinctually how to draw the audience in and had a knack for delivering new and refreshing information about wolves. The problem was that Shaman knew the very second Kent was not paying attention to him, and the wolf would take advantage of that. Shaman would help himself to some object belonging to an audience member or something in the room.

The sneaky wolf would grab a book bag or backpack sitting on the floor, or a hidden trash receptacle stashed behind a desk. The racket would disrupt the whole program. It was at that point I really began handling Shaman full time in the programs, allowing Kent to focus on the audience. I remember the first time I walked Shaman in front of a group of around 150 kids. The kids were all sitting quiet, listening to Kent talk about Shaman. As I walked out into the center of the room, I felt my anxiety level rise. Shaman focused his attention on the front row of students. I knew then that I needed to develop eagle eyes for Shaman. The best thing I could do to protect the wolf was never to take my eyes off of him, every moment we were in public.

As he walked along, I searched up ahead of him, looking for any loose backpacks or forgotten lunch sacks. Material objects that may entice the wolf's attention and create an aggressive, possessive response were to be avoided. It was becoming common for Shaman to vocalize his "Baaahhh" in front of an audience. Shaman's vocal cords had matured well beyond the simple communicative "Baaahhh" he started with into deep, full grizzly bear growls that easily rolled from his lips. He now walked around stiff and rigid with his fur standing up on all ends. He often held his head up, with his eyes wide and pupils flared. His lips vibrated against his impressive set of canine teeth. He was growing into one intense wolf.

Shaman vocalizing his possessive intentions over someone's backpack was not the message we wanted the public to take home with them. Our intent was to inspire people to care for wild wolves and the natural world in order to make a positive change for the better. The wolf program was not meant to perpetuate more fear toward the already misunderstood creature. Shaman's final public program took place in a large library. It was clear the big wolf should have stayed home, but before he completely retired to permanent residence, he would have one more day in the spotlight. The program was set in a room big enough to seat two hundred people; it quickly filled up and became standing room only long before the program even started. Interested people of all ages filled the room and eagerly waited for Shaman to make his appearance. When Kent was ready for the wolf to join, I quickly exited to get him. When I opened the door of the van, Shaman was excited and ready to get out. I double-checked the tension on the chain around his neck. Once I was satisfied Shaman was secured, we left the van and headed into the room. I briskly walked Shaman in and led him directly to the front of the room.

Once Shaman saw Kent, his whole demeanor changed. He began to puff himself up and pulled me in Kent's direction. I knew that it was not because Shaman wanted to greet Kent with happiness. Instead, it felt very much like he was saying with his drive and body language, "I am going to kick your butt!" And I had enough experience to know that I needed to steer the tough wolf away from Kent to avoid a confrontation. I worked to keep Shaman in the center of the room. That was challenging, because after the first walk and smell, Shaman lost interest in exploring and wanted to tell Kent off.

I continued to hold the big wolf back from Kent. But it became Shaman's focus to get to him. I spent several stressful moments turning Shaman away from Kent and circling him around on the small staged area. When I did, Shaman would immediately turn me back around toward Kent. Shaman knew what I was up to; he was not dumb, and he kept trying to override me. He almost got away with it too.

This was the final tour of the year, and we had done a great job avoiding any and all confrontations with Shaman. I did not want to blow the good reputation we were working hard to create. Both Kent and I wanted this to be a successful last appearance for the Shaman. He spent a lot of his time in a van, traveling to teach and inspire thousands of people about the nature of wolves and why they deserved protection in the wild. Shaman deserved nothing less than the best, regardless of his outbursts. Anyone entering into a relationship with a wolf would have to expect such behavior and accept it as the norm, or more problems with potentially devastating consciences could arise.

Shaman continued trying to drag me toward Kent. He pranced around like he owned the place, and me, for that matter; this was one of the most physically challenging programs I had done. At three years old, Shaman weighed close to 130 pounds, only slightly less than the 140 pounds I weighed. He was far more powerful than I was, and the only difference was that Shaman did not know his strength. It was all I could do to keep myself calm, remain confident, and stand strong in that small space with such a huge fiery presence. Kent was leaning up against a large table with his back toward us, talking to the audience. We had placed the table there specifically so Shaman could jump up and be seen by the people all the way in the back.

After ten minutes, Shaman began to relax his energy and the attention he was focusing on Kent. Until a few moments later, Kent turned his attention toward Shaman, asking me to bring him over and get him up on the table. A lightning bolt of anxiety went through the core of my being. I did not want to, after the intensity he was displaying toward Kent. But I agreed and walked over, briefly handed the lead to Kent, who turned back to the audience as Shaman eagerly jumped up on the table behind him. I could hear comments from the people in the back of the room, who could finally see him. With so many people in the room, it was hard to see Shaman. I could relate to that feeling, and we did the best we could to make Shaman visible to everyone. I looked around the audience while Shaman stood still on his perch for a few moments; I could see their attention was focused in fascination on the big black wolf.

I relaxed a bit. Maybe the wolf would behave better than I feared. Kent was focused on his words, and Shaman stood on the table, looking out into the audience. Without thinking, Kent reached his hand up to his food treat pocket and gently patted it. Shaman immediately took notice and thought he was getting a treat. He quickly came around Kent's back to his left side. Standing on the table made Shaman much taller and that much larger, and it put Kent at a great disadvantage. Shaman's nose and jaws were at the same height as Kent's flannel shirt pocket. The same pocket held lots of treats and smelled strongly of turkey kielbasa sausage and hot dogs.

Initially Shaman acted cool, I again took hold of the lead and gave Shaman a little slack, enough for the wolf to get around the front of Kent. Kent unconsciously folded the lip of his pocket back down and took his hand away without getting a treat out and rewarding Shaman. That was a big mistake. Midsentence, Kent was abruptly silenced and before either Kent or I could react, "Roar! Baaahhh!" Shaman scolded Kent right in front of the audience; clearly, the wolf was not pleased that he did not get a treat, as he expected. Up went his tail, hackles, and head. The room grew silent. No matter where we were, or whom we were in front of, Shaman felt no inhibitions to show us exactly what he was feeling toward Kent. And this was the most intense public display Shaman would have.

I quickly put pressure on the leash to reel him back towards me, but was met with strong resistance. Shaman seemed glued to the top of the table while Kent tried to deal with the hot head wolf and keep his own cool. I felt embarrassed for Kent and quickly figured out that I could use the slippery tabletop to my advantage. I slid Shaman off the table to the floor and led the fired-up wolf around in a circle behind Kent. I wanted to get him to calm back down again, or we would have to leave the room. Unfortunately, he would not calm down; it was clear he had a kielbasa to pick with Kent. And I decided it was best to end this appearance on a neutral note before anything more happened. I pulled the wolf out the door, after his final Ambassador performance, and back to the van we went.

Once I loaded the wolf back inside his kennel I got in and stayed with Shaman; I wanted to see how the wolf would react after his performance. After a few moments, he acted like nothing at all happened. It seemed his behaviors were clearly his natural, instinctual way of dealing with the humans in his life. There was nothing I could do to stop him from acting dominant, at least that I knew in that moment. And punishment or abuse on any level was out of the question. I would just as soon retire the wolf to enclosure life than raise a hand to him or any animal, and Kent felt the same too. I did not realize how upset I had gotten over this until I sat back in the van. I have to admit holding back a 130-pound wolf that wanted to challenge Kent in front of hundreds of people tops my list of the most nerve-racking moments in my life.

A moment to never repeat, and it took a few more moments to regain my composure before I could walk back into the building. All the noise that came out of the wolf and his peacock posturing had gotten my adrenaline pumping. Once my heart was back down in my chest and out of my throat, I walked back into the room. The room was charged with the energy Shaman had let out. Kent was surrounded by people and talking to two gentlemen in particular who had been in the back of the room during the presentation. They could not believe how calmly Kent stood with Shaman in his face like a mad grizzly bear. Kent did keep his composure, and that impressed them. They even said that from the back of the room, they were scared for Kent.

I have to acknowledge my part in the downfall of Shaman's public life; at least once I learned what my part was. In my formative years working with wolves, I was amused by the antics between Shaman and Kent. The fact that Shaman would challenge Kent for me was flattering in a way. And without realizing it, I encouraged this behavior to continue and worsen. Yes, I was guilty of not knowing how to raise a wolf with a wild mind like Shaman's to believe I was a worthy leader. And laughing at Shaman when he became loud and boisterous toward Kent accelerated his advances toward the man. The door was about to swing open on learning just how important the way I felt, my emotions, my energy played in my connection to the wolf, and I needed to get my head out before it got slammed when the door swung shut.

Back at the sanctuary, I began to see that Shaman perceived me as his property. His actions were not unlike that of a jealous boyfriend, and whenever I was present, challenging sparks continued to flare between Kent and Shaman. However, Kent did not take any of Shaman's disrespectful advances personally. In fact, he worked through them, and as long as I stayed away, his relationship with Shaman remained just fine. I believed this was admirable, because other people in this position could have become too afraid to work with the animal, possibly even having Shaman put to death. Not Kent, he accepted Shaman for what he was, and that was that.

The following summer, 1992, two more homeless wolf pups came to live at the sanctuary. As part of Shaman's retirement, he occasionally babysat these wolf pups. He was the perfect role model, schooling the pups, and they quickly grew to adore the big wolf. One day, Kent brought a group of Boy Scouts up the hill to see the pups. They stood outside of the enclosure where Shaman and the pups were hanging out. It was not Shaman's regular enclosure; it was the puppy pen (earlier, I had opened the gate and let Shaman in with the pups). Kent wanted the Boy Scouts to meet the new arrivals, and he knew Shaman was babysitting them that day. I heard the group walking up the path from the chair in my cabin. Kent walked into the entrance of the enclosure and called out to the pups to get their attention and come meet the visitors. From my desk I heard Kent calling out. The pups were all sleeping in the shade under the cabin; it was a hot July afternoon.

I heard the pups wake up underneath our cabin and excitedly run out to see Kent; they were so little and people friendly. Shaman's attention went to Kent also, and like a giant puppy, he ran down to see Kent. When I stepped out on the porch, I saw Kent readying to meet the puppies and a protective Shaman, who had decided to guard the pups from Kent. I could hear Shaman's trademark grizzly bear tone and felt trouble brewing. Shaman and Kent reached the pups at about the same time. I stepped off the porch just as Shaman mouthed Kent's hand and punctured a hole deep enough to bleed. I grabbed a towel from my desk, walked out, and handed it to Kent. Shaman's disposition immediately changed when he saw me, and he became like a big puppy again.

I distracted Shaman enough to get him to follow me down the hill to the gate of his enclosure. He happily bounded down behind me through the entry and away from the pups, his tail undecided whether it should be wagging in happiness or flagged as if he were the king. Kent then walked down with the two happy little wolf pups, eager to greet the kids.

CHAPTER 13

Rooftop Rescue

It did not take long for the wolves to discover that they could jump up onto the slope of the roof and climb to the top.

Nearly a year after little Sila arrived at MW, Peaches came to live at the sanctuary. This pup was very special; an entire book could be written just about her. But for the sake of keeping this book smaller than a dictionary, I will only include one short but profound story about her. My son Tamas was only ten years old when Peaches came into his life. This highly intuitive wolf was five weeks old and a little bundle of energy. She immediately adored Tamas, and the two would grow up together.

One day, Kent and I woke up at sunrise, loaded up the van, and traveled out to run errands in the city for the day. Tamas wanted to stay home and did not want to go to town with us, so he stayed back with the others to participate in that day's activities. Young Peaches lived in the Ambassador wolf enclosure, right up next to the community building. The roof of the community building sloped down toward the ground and reached inside the wolf enclosure, with the wooden edge standing only a couple of feet from the ground. It did not take long for the wolves to discover that they could jump up onto the slope of the roof and climb to the top. But in order to get up on the roof, they needed a running start to leap up onto the edge.

Once they became comfortable climbing on the edge, the wolves would quickly sprint up the side, using the rough shingles as traction. Once on top of the roof, they would spend hours lounging and scrutinizing whatever went on in the parking lot and in the other wolf enclosures. The rooftop proved to be the ultimate vantage point; the wolves could see practically everything going on at the sanctuary, especially in the parking lot, where carcasses of dead animals arrived, were cut up into smaller pieces, and carried to all the different enclosures. At night, it was challenging to sleep inside the building, because the sleeping loft was set directly under the rooftop pathway the wolves used. From inside the building, it sounded like a herd of horses galloping up the side of the house, and this often woke me up.

A year after Peaches arrived, we took in three more homeless wolves: Hina, Jazmine, and Bowdi. The three youngsters had been introduced into the big wolf pen, with Lucus's pack in the enclosure nearest to where Peaches lived. That fall, as breeding season was just around the corner, we again needed to separate the males from the females. Lots of work was continually being done to improve the enclosures. The fences were expanded when the population of homeless wolves grew. Raven and Jordan did not easily accept the new female arrivals. And the center of Raven and Jordan's focus was directed at young Hina.

Hina spent a lot of time inside the den, until one day the fighting between the females escalated and resulted in a big hole on Hina's leg. Raven did not show any signs of letting up on her wrath toward Hina either, so we temporarily moved Hina out of the big wolf pen. It seemed a good time for a break, while Raven and Jordan were in the height of estrus. Simultaneously, construction was being done on the enclosure that Hina had been temporarily moved to, located adjacent to the big wolf pen. There it would be quiet and safe for the young wolf to recover, and after enough time passed, we could determine if Hina should go back into the big wolf pen.

We returned from our long journey well after dark, and as we pulled into the parking lot, everyone at the sanctuary was asleep. All was silent except for a few wolves that came to the fence lines as we walked up the path to our cabin. The next morning, we awoke to Tamas standing at the foot of the bed, and he was excited to tell us what happened during our absence the day before. The gate to Hina's temporary enclosure had been left unlatched by a caretaker taking a break from construction. When the gate swung open, young Hina wandered out of her enclosure and was loose in the front yard. I sat straight up in bed; one of the worst nightmares for us was to have the wolves loose for any reason. Certainly running loose was a death sentence for the animal, especially if it wandered off the sanctuary grounds and scared an unsuspecting neighbor. As Tamas described how everyone freaked out, worried that Hina would run away, I felt an intense fear; was she still out?

Anxiety popped up in my stomach, and I wanted to ask if Hina was okay, but I held my words and continued to listen.

"Everyone was afraid that if they went out to try to catch Hina, they would scare her," Tamas explained. He was the only person there who had a bond with Hina, and the only person Hina was not afraid to come up to. The caretakers were all gathered in the community kitchen for lunch when one of them looked out the window and saw Hina wandering around the grounds. Everyone was afraid to doing anything for fear they would make the problem worse.

That's when they looked at Tamas. As they watched Hina sniffing around the front yard, they decided to give Tamas the leash and send him out the door to catch Hina and take her back into the enclosure. That was a big job for a ten-year-old boy to do. Catch and leash a shy, ninety-pound yearling wolf that had never been leash trained. Tamas was reluctant to try; even though Hina had grown to trust the boy in the few months she had known him. He said that as he left the porch, lead in hand, he noticed Peaches along with other wolves gathered on top the roof, watching Hina wander around the front from about a hundred yards away.

When Hina saw Tamas walking out toward her, she became excited and seemed glad to have a friend out in the front yard, which gave her security. She ran up to Tamas, jumping up on him as he made contact with her. She even gave him a couple of licks on his face, but when she saw the leash in his hand, she became suspicious and was not about to let him touch her with it, never mind put it around her neck. She probably felt his discomfort about it too and reflected that, in addition to her own fear. The caretakers had moved to the porch and watched helplessly as Tamas continued to try to get Hina to come to him. Shouting and cursing filled the airspace, and Tamas could not catch Hina. All this time, the three wolves on the roof were howling and carrying on, watching the antics.

The shouting made Tamas more nervous, and whenever Tamas was close enough to try to put a leash on Hina, she would dodge it and quickly move away. Then something completely unexpected happened; Hina began to move farther away from Tamas, and the staff became more frantic. Without warning, a loud noise came from the roof of the community building: "Bang, bang, bang!" As the astonished staff watched, Peaches jumped down off the backside of the rooftop. Landing first on the space between the loft roof, and then on to the community trailer roof. Finally, Peaches jumped one more level down, where she reached the ground.

To everyone's astonishment, Peaches did not mess around; she immediately ran out to where Tamas was standing, ran straight past him, and confronted Hina, grabbing her in her teeth. Once Peaches had a grip on Hina, she rolled the confused yearling upside down at Tamas's feet. When she did, Hina tucked her tail up tight against her belly and obeyed Peaches, running back inside her enclosure.

"Peaches put Hina back in the pen," Tamas exclaimed.

Once she did, a somewhat confused and bewildered Tamas was able to make it to the gate with Hina in and Peaches out, quickly slamming the gate shut.

Peaches, clearly proud of herself, strutted back up the hill and quickly made her way to her own enclosure gate entry. There she was easily let back in with her pack by one of the caretakers waiting on the porch. We were told that Peaches did receive a few appreciation pets and praises from some amazed people before they let her back in. I sat back in my bed as Tamas finished telling us; puzzled and amazed, it raised questions in my mind. A short bit later, I walked down to the community building and was greeted by a few of the caretakers, still buzzing by the past day's events. Everyone was amazed at what had happened, and some speculation occurred as well.

Could Peaches read our minds enough to know that Tamas needed help? Was it just coincidence, or was it something else such as his nervous body language? Later that day, we devised a test to see if Peaches would jump off the roof again, now that she knew a way out of her enclosure. She had never jumped off the roof before, and she had been at MW nearly two years, running up and down that roof. To add to the enticement, the smell of the compost pile was out back in the same area. Even with that temptation, she still had not jumped.

We placed a road-kill deer on the ground near where she had gotten out. We watched from a distance and waited to see if it would entice her to jump, but to no avail. A couple days later, however, she led the other wolves on a rooftop escape expedition into the fully enclosed recycling area. There they found a treasure-trove of recycling cans, cartons, and trash, and we found the three eagerly rummaging through any leftovers they could find, leaving a torn-up mess. And because she had set a pretty clear example for the other wolves to get off the roof, we installed a piece of fence across the edge of the rooftop to prevent future mishaps. As for speculation about why this happened, I chose to believe in the intuitive connection that we were sharing with the wolves.

Peaches and Tracy wait outside a local Colorado
school. Photograph courtesy Jan Frye Pinner.

CHAPTER 14

Heart String Connections

As I grabbed hold of Noya's thick neck fur, I felt a surge of tremendous pressure and sadness come through my body.

It was August of 1995 when a freak event happened to me at the sanctuary. It was the most profound intuitive connection I had experienced with a wolf to date. One sunny summer day, I gathered together with friends who were helping me complete a writing project I was having trouble with. We met inside one of the tipis and were well on our way through several sheets of paper when lunchtime came up, and we decided to take a break to eat. I skipped lunch to better organize the notes; that way, I could be more productive when my friends returned. As I sat there reading and re-reading, I began wondering what I was trying to portray in this story in the first place, when out of the blue, I heard a voice in the distance, screaming for help.

The sound was so alarming, the hair stood up on the back of my neck. I immediately jumped up, threw my papers aside, and rushed to the entryway. I stopped and hesitated, listening carefully, trying to figure out which direction the cry for help was coming. At that same time, a group of students had just arrived from overseas to stay a few weeks as part of a work-and-peace camp. The purpose of the camp was that people from different cultures came together for a few weeks out of the year and created something positive. Earlier, I had seen the students out exploring the sanctuary grounds; was that cry for help one of them? A frightful feeling ran up my spine as I wondered whether one of the students had unknowingly entered a wolf pen.

Many of the fourteen campers understood little to no English, and it was a challenge to communicate simple sentences; surely it was clear that no one should enter the wolf enclosures, but I needed to be sure that everyone was where they were supposed to be. Again the scream came: "Help!" This time, without hesitation, I jumped through the tipi door flap and headed downward toward the lower enclosures, where I believed the cry originated. As I reached the first perimeter gate, to my surprise, the gate was closed and latched.

I stopped and looked around and found no sign of any human out of place. My heart was pounding in my throat as the vocal came again: "Help!" I grew nauseous as I frantically looked around for the source of the screams. I could see the international students up on the hill, quite a ways from the wolves, setting up their campsites. Thank goodness! I could rule out one of them being in trouble. A slight wave of relief flowed through me, and now I felt a wolf and not a person crying out for help. I looked around for any other staff; I was the only one in the lower wolf habitat. No one else was around.

Most of the volunteer staff had gone inside to eat lunch, and no one else seemed concerned or even reacted to the cries for help. I grew confused and wondered if I was hearing things. It appeared I was the only one reacting to the scream. I went through the gate and latched it behind me. Quieting down, I listened again, wondering where the cries were coming from. I could hear a couple of people walking toward the community building above where I was walking. Then the loudest and clearest cry came: "Help!" How could no one else hear that?

This time, I could tell it was coming from the lowest wolf enclosure. I started running down the path in the direction of the cry. As I ran, I could see the wolves standing at attention along each fence line. They appeared as concerned as I was; they too had heard the cries and were looking intently at the lowest enclosure in the little aspen grove. I found that reassuring and knew I was headed in the right direction. I raced down the hill until I was standing in front of the lowest gate. I reached my hand out to open the gate latch. Just then, I heard the cry again, and I knew it was Noya. Her howl was always music to my ears, and her voice was unique. It sounded ethereal, like the voice of an angel.

Noya sounded stressed, as if she was hurt or caught in something. As I got close, I realized that the sound I was hearing was not her beautiful, angelic howl. I quickly opened the entry gate and walked inside. I could see her canine companions, Raku and Yaqui, sitting higher up the hill, looking down into a patch of scrub oak and brush. The wolves had been fed a butchered cow earlier that day, and many of them were guarding their leftovers. I was surprised to see that nobody else in the enclosure seemed concerned about Noya, including Rogue, a new puppy addition. I thought that was unusual; Noya always attracted attention from the other canines. I called out to Noya; the green foliage was so thick, it was impossible to see her. I felt like I had entered an untrimmed, rundown maze of scrub oak. Searching with my eyes, I kept listening for her voice; a cold silent feeling filled my heart. I was scared; where was little Noya, the most unusual wolf at the sanctuary? She was unique and special. I felt a deep love for Noya; she was different from the others in many ways.

I did not know if Noya howled as a puppy before her head injury, and I can only assume. But somewhere along the line, it seemed she had lost her howl. From the time of my arrival to the sanctuary to Noya's third year, she kept silent. Sometime after she turned three years old, she began to howl. And when Noya finally did howl, it was unforgettable, otherworldly, and beautiful. Noya's voice was strong and feminine, with a higher pitch than the other female wolves at the sanctuary. A unique sound all her own. To me, it was the most beautiful wolf howl I had ever heard or ever will hear. No matter where I stood at the sanctuary, when the wolves howled, I could always pick out Noya.

The scrub oak rattled as a few short, pained yelps came from inside the brush. I searched for Noya with my eyes and still could not see her. I called out loudly to her; this time, the scrub oak shook. Its tiny leaves rocked back and forth. Noya must have heard my voice. She finally emerged from the thick scrub and pushed her way toward me. I was horrified at what I saw: Sweet Noya was bloated up so big and hard that her belly was huge and round. I reached down to touch and comfort her, and my blood ran cold when I realized I could not feel her backbone because she was so bloated.

I immediately recognized this was deathly serious. A rise of despair came out of me as I screamed out at the top of my lungs: "Help! Help! Help!" Finally, someone up the hill heard me screaming and came running down to help. "Noya is dying!" I cried.

I yelled up for them to bring the car and find Kent. I wasn't prepared for this and did not see it coming. I had no idea what to do and became panic stricken. Oh my God, I thought to myself, and then realized the best way to help my friend in her time of extreme need was to stay calm. She had called me for help and I came. I stood there, knowing Noya was dying, and we did not have much time. My intuition told me there was nothing I could do except drop down and be with her. I knew I had to stay with her.

Searching for relief, Noya pushed her head into my stomach. I reached out with my hands to try and comfort her. As I grabbed hold of Noya's thick neck fur, I felt a surge of tremendous pressure and sadness jolt my body. I was afraid to touch her belly. I thought that if I massaged her head, it might distract her from the pain she was feeling. I gently took hold of her head and began rubbing as I talked to her through my tears. At that moment, I understood there was far more to wolves than I ever imagined.

Wolves had many more levels of being than I had read about in any book, and few words touched on their intuitive essence. The energy I was feeling in that moment of Noya's good-bye was deeply heartbreaking. As I continued to hold Noya, I thanked her and told her what an incredible animal she was and how much I loved her.

Noya helped me realize just how strong the intuitive connection between wolf and human could be.

Apparently, during feeding, Noya ate, or rather inhaled like a vacuum, large pieces of raw meat that were intended to be chewed and swallowed, stuffing herself like a gluttonous pig.

This could have been in response to a recent change in the dynamics of her pack; Rogue had been introduced to Noya's enclosure at only six months old. Noya was nine years old, and her digestive tract could not handle this sudden surge of an overabundance of meat. Something had gone horribly wrong in the process. She looked up at me, and I could see the pressure and pain in her eyes. I cried out, and I did not know what else to do as we waited for the car to come and rush Noya to the vet. I knew in my heart that Noya had called me to say good-bye. Tears poured down my cheeks; I could not hold back the sadness I was feeling.

We did not expect to lose the little wolf I had grown so attached to. A few moments later, the car made it down the hill, but it was too late. Noya's spirit seemed gone, and she had become despondent. The late-night run to the emergency vet failed, and early the following morning, Noya's body finally quit. When Noya left me, she made me recognize the gift of connection I had with these incredible creatures. Holding her close for those precious few last moments is a memory I will never forget.

CHAPTER 15

"Whisper," Says the Eagle

The same morning Whisper's pups were discovered, a golden eagle appeared.

Shortly after Noya's burial, my attention turned to Zephyr. Due to his vindictive nature towards his elders, and the sisters, we decided to move him into an enclosure that was near the big wolf pen. After a short period of acclimation in his new habitat, three young wolves named Crazy Horse, Whisper, and Aspen joined Zephyr. From there, antics began to brew in his newly formed pack. With the seasons changing, fall brought out high energy in the canines, not only because of the colder weather, but sparked by hormonal changes. Breeding season was not far away, and it seemed when one or more of the wolves were feeling frisky, the wave of energy would quickly pass through the rest of the wolf packs. Pretty soon, everyone's attitude had shifted.

Bickering about simple things such as food, bones, or the attention of human friends seemed to be the predominant activity. As their caretakers, usually, the topic of discussion that day evolved around the wolf pack behaviors and it was usually the pups that created the ruckus. Because Zephyr was still getting used to the young wolves living in the pen with him, at first he showed little aggression towards them. Often they annoyed him to the point he would run away and seek solitude.

It was interesting to stand back and compare the behaviors of Lucus' pack next to Zephyr's from a distance. The two most prominent wolf packs living next to each other, there were varied amount of personalities interacting. Lucus, Raven, Jordan and Nikkolah had been loyal companions from puppyhood, with little to no consideration for fighting that resulted in injury; occasionally they would fight until one was seriously injured, but for the most part, the energy was consistent in that wolf pack.

One day, I watched the behaviors between the big wolf pen and Zephyr's recently formed pack. Since the passing of Cyndar, Zephyr often ran away and evaded the elder wolves in his final weeks as part of the big wolf pack. I loved to compare in my mind Zephyr, Whisper, Crazy Horse, and Aspen to the seemingly functional state of Lucus's pack. Zephyr had not yet taken hold of leadership or established himself in any way with the young wolves.

He might not have understood how to, or he might not even have recognized he should. Whisper, the only female in the pack, acted more like an alpha than Zephyr, and that was unusual because she was still an adolescent, nearing her second year of life, and Zephyr was full grown. What an explosive time in the history of this pack. As long as Aspen and Crazy Horse showed submission to Whisper, they seemed to get along fine. Zephyr continued as best he could to avoid the young wolves, but they so desperately wanted his acknowledgment and attention. His reaction to the three curious and eager young wolves: "Leave me alone."

If they continued to pursue him, Zephyr would become agitated, or if either Crazy Horse or Aspen felt like dominating Whisper, that would start the fighting. The fighting and screaming that came from those three was enough to make you sit straight up and pay attention, and I did. Whisper adored Zephyr; even so, for the most part, he continued to completely ignore her advances. It turned out that for Whisper, being ignored by Zephyr was like an aphrodisiac.

It drove her to pursue him even more, which brought on even more fighting between Zephyr's pack mates.

Zephyr's pack lived among several of the largest trees at the sanctuary. A natural spring bubbled in the lowest part of the valley, providing a water pond during the wet summer months. At the top between the trees was a small but lovely meadow; this clearing would become a favorite place for the wolves to hang out. From there, they had a terrific view of what went on in Lucus's enclosure.

And that is how they spent most of their time: watching one another. The wolves had a vantage point for watching what some of the people were doing too. Whenever I would enter the pen, the wolves would come running to see me momentarily, but then they would head back up to their vantage point to resume watching. I thought how much that behavior reminded me of watching television. Only better: Wolf TV had a positive effect on me, and no annoying commercials. The wolves were so enthralled to watch what was going in their neighbor's enclosure, they lost track that I was standing right there.

When something occurred between Nikkolah, Bowdi and Lucus, it created a reaction in the big wolf pack. Watching frantically from the opposite pen, Zephyr, Whisper, Aspen, and Crazy Horse would race up to the top of the meadow clearing. It was there Zephyr's pack could best witness the goings-on of Lucus and Nikkolah from a distance, inside a heavily wooded enclosure. The four would stop under the large ponderosa pine tree, where they would freeze. Standing completely still, they became so quiet you could hear a pin drop. Silently, they stood as if holding their breath not to miss a single sound. Their eyes wide open, unblinking in anticipation of the next move.

The wolves would go back and forth, depending on the action happening in the opposite enclosure (like changing channels on a television). Zephyr seemed to be most interested in the Nikkolah channel. Maybe that was a leftover desire to kick Nikkolah's butt, like he used to do when he was much younger, living in the big wolf pen. The wolves never seemed to tire of watching the other pack's life happening next door. Back and forth along the fence line they would run, watching each other, mirroring exact behaviors through the fence. If Nikkolah was being dominated in the big wolf pen, Zephyr would dominate Whisper, Aspen, or Crazy Horse, depending on who was the closest available. Shrill screaming could be heard all around the refuge during these times.

Other wolves in nearby enclosures wanted to see what the excitement was. I could see their heads bobbing up and down like the most zealous television viewers. They were often so noisy during the night I would sit straight up in bed, worried they were killing one another. If I felt concerned enough to get out of bed and go outside into the night and look, I would usually see that the disruption was a whole lot of noise and not much else: wolves jumping up and displaying body language to the other wolves.

I was fascinated to see the wolves watch each other and mirror one another's behavior. It was entertaining to watch Zephyr and Nikkolah go back and forth; they were by far the most animated about it. When the wolves would tire and go on to something else, Nikkolah would get miffed and take it out on Bowdi. He would dominate Bowdi more loudly and actively than Lucus would, as if he was showing off to Zephyr. Zephyr watched enthralled at every move Nikkolah would make. Zephyr would bellow and howl, like an enthusiastic fan booing the opposing team after a score. If Aspen, Crazy Horse, or Whisper were within Zephyr's reach, they would soon learn just how much of a poor sport he was when it came to Nikkolah's activities.

In human terms, Zephyr would take out his lack of team spirit on them. As I watched those behaviors day to day, I could see clearly that Zephyr and Nikkolah continued to kick each other's butts long-distance. It was humorous to watch the two walking around their enclosures; all puffed up like peacocks, two tough boys that used the fence as a safety net. Retaining a safe distance from one another allowed each to keep his high opinion of himself and own worldly status intact. The females were as animated as the males were performing for one another. They too were constantly tuned into one another's whereabouts.

Whisper's favorite was the Hina channel. She never seemed to miss an episode, similar to a faithful TV soap watcher. Whisper and Hina were potential rivals, and the proximity of their fences made for the same behaviors and body posturing as Zephyr and Nikkolah. Air posturing was the only way I could describe the communications going on between the two at a distance. When Whisper mimicked Hina, her gestures made it look like she was having a random temper tantrum; she also made "air" movements, similar to someone playing air guitar. But with no other females living in the enclosure for Whisper to vent on, she would lay into Crazy Horse as her punching (or rather biting) bag. It was a rare occasion that Aspen got nailed by Whisper. He had no problem resting under the trees, minding his own business, watching the displays from a good distance away and avoiding all conflicts.

In the deep cold of winter, Zephyr began to take a romantic interest in Whisper (at least as romantic as a wolf gets). The two of them begin to frolic together; caretakers frequently observed the social interaction between the wolves. For the first time, Zephyr became protective of Whisper, guarding her openly from Crazy Horse. Because Whisper was in her estrus cycle, that could attract undesired attention from the unfixed Crazy Horse.

The year prior we planned that by getting vasectomy surgeries done, we would no longer need to separate the males from the females during the breeding season. We blow-darted Aspen and Zephyr with a tranquilizer for their procedures, and Crazy Horse became terrified after witnessing them being carried out of their enclosure on a stretcher. He became overly afraid, and adrenaline charged; he completely lost it.

In full flight mode, Crazy Horse ran throughout his enclosure so fast that the darts I fired at him went in and quickly popped back out. The little fluid that did penetrate his fur and skin wore off quickly. Not wanting to stress him any longer than necessary after the short failed attempt, we decided to leave him be for the time being and work to vasectomize him before the next season. Until then, Crazy Horse remained fully intact.

After a couple of days passed by, concern rose inside of me, when I learned Crazy Horse seemed more obsessed with Whisper. Although Zephyr stayed by Whisper's side, it was only my belief in a theory from a book I had seen, about wild alpha wolf pairs being monogamous through out their lifetimes. For the time being, using this excuse as a basis for why Whisper would not solicit Crazy Horse gave me some relief. And I went on hope and a prayer that Whisper would not breed with Crazy Horse, especially after all the aggression she displayed toward him.

Whisper made it a regular practice to discipline Crazy Horse; she would barely tolerate his presence. Zephyr would frequently dominate Crazy Horse too. Regardless of how often the young male was chastised by Whisper and Zephyr, Crazy Horse was not dissuaded to keep trying. He followed the pair around constantly, waiting in the wings for his turn. During a visit with Whisper and the others, I noticed tiny, little bite marks on Crazy Horse's nose and face. His nose was like a pincushion from Whisper's teeth. On several occasions, Zephyr was seen trying (with no success) to mount Whisper.

Zephyr would jump up on her back, but he soon slid off without making any connection, and then he would repeat himself. He spent a lot of time sweetly licking her, all over her body and face. In all the times he was seen trying to mount Whisper, there was only once he came close to actually making contact. Traditional observations of wolves in the wild had often shown that subordinate wolves respected the alphas, and it was the alpha male and female that decided if any other pack mates would be allowed to breed. In this case, Zephyr appeared to be having difficulties getting respect from Crazy Horse.

We assumed that Zephyr would continue to keep Crazy Horse away from Whisper until she was out of her estrus cycle. Unfortunately, Zephyr was not living up to his end of the bargain. Because he was vasectomized, it made sense that his attempts at making a connection with Whisper continually failed. When I watched Whisper and Crazy Horse together, it did not seem very likely that the two would mate, ever. Every signal that Whisper gave to Crazy Horse was "No!" It was certainly an amusing time for all of us living at the sanctuary, experiencing these wild behaviors happening around us.

We watched as Zephyr Whisper, and Crazy Horse frequently went round and round in spats. Zephyr followed Whisper's every move, even going as far as walking by her side, and Crazy Horse followed both of them. It seemed that no matter how hard Zephyr tried, his constant attention to Whisper (or more accurately his failures to mount her) began to bore Whisper. There were signs that Whisper was losing interest. One time, I laughed as I watched Zephyr work hard, doing his best to get up on top of Whisper. All the while Whisper never stopped chewing on a bone, head down to the ground, not missing a crunch or even fazed by Zephyr's very existence. As the night passed, it was filled with fever-pitched howling and activity throughout the entire wolf valley.

I assumed that Zephyr and Whisper were doing their thing all night. And in fact, early the next morning, after all the commotion from the midnight noise we saw Crazy Horse and Whisper stuck butt to butt, plain as the light of day! The dreaded puppy making potential was happening right in front of us they had mated. Apparently, when it time came for Whisper to get serious about getting pregnant and fulfilling her need to reproduce, she knew what wolf could get the job done. And Whisper was willing to make exceptions for the seemingly lowly Crazy Horse.

Two months later, all the signs of having puppies were there. Whispers belly was swollen and hung heavy to the ground. She was pulling the fur from her teats striping her belly naked. Her emotions seemed heightened too, she was much more sensitive to everything. But she had not yet selected a den site, at least one that I was aware of.

One morning, I was up early, eager to see Whisper and check on Hina and Jazmine. On this particular morning, clean white snow lay on the ground. The air was wonderfully cold and sweet, and my breath jumped out ahead of me as I walked briskly down the path. The sanctuary was quiet. Everywhere I walked on the paths fresh snow, untouched by any living thing, blanketed the quiet wolf enclosures. As I reached Hina and Jazmine's enclosure, I looked beyond, up where Whisper lived, and noticed I could not see her anywhere.

As I walked across the ravine toward Zephyr's enclosure, I passed the two sisters, Hina and Jazmine were standing at the gate, wagging their tails at me, but for the time being, they would have to wait. I continued past their enclosure to see Whisper first; her belly was so heavy, and she could give birth any day. What caught my attention was I could see Crazy Horse running up the hill in a funny way. Zephyr seemed to be doing his normal behavior down the hill, watching the people in the parking lot. Crazy Horse, however, was acting sneaky, like he was stalking something up the hill and he did not want anyone to see him approaching. As I entered the enclosure, there was no sign of Whisper.

The lack of her strong presence gave me a funny feeling, because she was always there to greet me. I walked around, looking in the places I knew the dens were, and oddly enough, there was no sign in the snow at any of the entrances of the den sites, and no sound anywhere. I scanned the ground for any disruption of the dirt. Crazy Horse's behavior again caught my attention. I decided to walk to the top of the enclosure, where something had caught Crazy Horse's attention. As I climbed the hill, he came running down to greet me. His demeanor was different; he was reserved and on guard. I continued making my way up to the top of a large natural habitat enclosure when I noticed that Crazy Horse had stopped following me.

I turned and looked back at him; he stood there watching me as if he'd come to some invisible boundary line that he was not allowed to pass. Then I saw her: Whisper was under a tree, which puzzled me. She saw me coming and came to greet me, and then I heard little squeaks coming from under her. When I reached the spot, I saw tiny little pups, all tucked together in the snow at the base of the tree trunk. Whisper was excited, jumping up into my face, greeting me as I looked down at her pups. Zephyr and Crazy Horse stood watching in the distance, curious about what was going on under the tree. With all of Whisper's energy right in my face, it was hard to get a count of pups. I wondered why Whisper did not go into a den and give birth; did I mention the time of year? It was in April. The weather was winter conditions, still freezing and snowing, hardly temperatures suitable for newborn infant wolves. I walked away believing that I counted five little black and gray bodies, moving around at the base of that tree trunk. The day started to warm up, and I hoped it would stay warm for the sake of the pups.

Zephyr followed me as I walked out of the enclosure, and then he went chasing after Crazy Horse. As I walked back up the hill toward Hina and Jazmine's home, I turned and looked at the tree where Whisper nestled with her pups. To my surprise, she had left the pups and was now was standing at the fence line, watching me walk away and looking at Hina and Jazmine. I knew right then that Whisper's pups were in trouble. The same morning Whisper's pups were discovered, a large golden eagle appeared, and it landed in a tall ponderosa tree inside her enclosure. I spotted the eagle a few hours after I'd found the pups, and I watched the eagle, considering what its intent was. I wondered if it were waiting for an opportune time to swoop off with a puppy.

In the wild, it is not unheard of for eagles to predate on wolf puppies. Great! Another reason to worry. For the rest of the day, I watched the eagle from the kitchen trailer; I checked on the pups a couple of times, too. That whole day, the eagle did not move; it sat, stoic, in its perch on a large branch thirty feet up. I wanted to photograph the eagle, so I carried my camera down to Whisper's enclosure and walked up to the base of the tree where the eagle sat. I pointed my camera up and began to shoot photos. As I did, to my surprise and amusement, the eagle stood up off its perch, lifting his huge talons from the branch, and turned around, putting its back to me. I laughed and wondered if he just turned around because of me, like a reluctant celebrity ignoring my attempt to take a photo.

Nnnoooo! That was a coincidence; it must be! I walked around to the other side of the tree, lifted my camera, and pointed it back up at the bird. Again, the eagle stood up from its sitting position and blatantly turned its back to me. "What is that eagle doing?" I questioned Aspen out loud; he had wandered over to see what I was doing and noticed the large bird I was looking at.

Probably for his betterment, he was removed emotionally from the interactions going on with Zephyr, Crazy Horse, and Whisper. He seemed curious about the eagle too. Again I walked around to the other side of the tree to face the eagle, and without hesitation it did a third about-face. It was definitely sending me a clear message that it did not want me in its view, as if I would go away just because he could not see me. This behavior tickled me, until I remembered why the eagle was potentially there. The eagle made me nervous just hanging out in a tree branch of the enclosure. Perched a short distance away from an inexperienced momma wolf, and her vulnerable infant puppies. The eagle was stubborn, too, or at least it appeared that way to me.

It was odd that it did not fly off when I was standing just below it on the ground, walking circles around the trunk of a ponderosa pine tree that seemed a hundred feet tall. Loudly talking to it, snapping photos of it, and I wasn't the only creature annoyed by the presence of an eagle. Come to think of it, on any other occasion, I would be honored to spend time in the presence of such a magnificent creature, but now was not that time. Six of the local ravens that lived in and around the wolf enclosure pestered and dive-bombed the eagle; the ravens seemed to take turns and were relentless, at least the first day.

The actions of the raven birds did not affect the eagle in the slightest bit; it remained unshaken, almost catatonic, fixed to the branch well into the next day. The ravens did not give up easily either (or quickly, for that matter). They circled the aspen forest in protest of the presence of the bird of prey. It did not seem to matter to the eagle if the ravens flew around picking on him, all day and night. Unaffected, the eagle remained sitting. After twenty-four hours of consistent pestering and only being ignored, the ravens finally retreated back to their trees. Whisper stayed under the tree most of the first two days after her pups arrived. When I checked the tree early the following morning, I found Whisper just where she should be.

The eagle remained fixed like a stone statue on its perch, a slight distance from the newborns. A light snow overnight had covered the ground with a fresh white blanket. It looked like Whisper had not left her pups all night; that was good. The snow was undisturbed except for one set of tracks that circled around the base of the tree's perimeter. Odd, I thought before I became sidetracked by Whisper's eager greeting. When I bent down to give a greeting to Whisper and to check the pups, I could hear their little voices and see some wiggling. With Whisper's tongue licking the side of my face, I counted the pups. I could see one, two, three puppies, and then four, but number five was missing; where was number five?

I stood up and looked all around; no sign of the fifth pup. A twinge of panic clutched at my stomach as I continued to search for the missing pup. There was no sign of any disturbance, only a simple circle one time around the diameter of the tree from some curious bird. One of the pups was missing. The eagle remained firmly planted in the tree; prior to this, eagles had frequently flown over the sanctuary, but rarely had we received a visit such as this. The interested ravens that had gathered in nearby trees kept their eye on the eagle and probably Whisper and her pups too. The temperatures remained cold, freezing at night, and the snow was melting very slowly.

Concerned the remaining pups were going to disappear or die, I did not know what to do. It almost seemed the novelty of having pups was wearing off for Whisper. She was more interested in what was going on with Hina and Jazmine, or with Raven and Jordan, than in what was going on under a special tree in her enclosure. Early on the next morning, I found her on the hill, watching me as I hurried down to see her. An alarm went off in my head. Whisper was so young, just a year old herself, and she'd had no role model to show her how to nurture pups or prompt her to be motherly. It appeared Whisper had resumed her obsession to discipline Crazy Horse.

Crazy Horse was curious about the pups, and he wanted so badly to sneak in under the tree and see them, but there was no way Whisper would allow him. He spent most of his day prodding and pushing her, violating her space limits with his frequent attempts. Whisper spent most of her day running him around, chasing after Crazy Horse, and chastising Zephyr too. Whisper had little time for Wolf TV, or air challenging her neighbor Hina, at least in the first few days. Whisper had not given birth to the pups in a den dug into the ground, which meant she had a lot more work to do; she expended a lot of energy keeping track of them. Whisper seemed sharp, at least when it came to Zephyr and Crazy Horse. She could always be one step ahead of the two boys if she wanted to, no matter where in the enclosure she was.

It was interesting to see her reaction to the boys; once, I watched both Zephyr and Crazy Horse run up the hill to check out the puppies under the tree when they knew Whisper was distracted. She was on the other side of the enclosure, growling at Hina through the fence. Hina was in a spat with her sister Jazmine, over a hunk of meat or something. Once Whisper caught on to the fact that the boys headed toward the tree, and they were closer to her pups than she was, she threw a vocal fit. She roared up at them, throwing her voice at them like a ventriloquist. And even from a distance, they stopped in their tracks and promptly turned back around, ignoring Whisper. The two sheepishly pretended as if they were not doing anything but innocently walking past the puppy nest.

The eagle was still in its tree, and the ravens had disappeared. A huge sense of apprehension settled over me, as I feared that I would have to play God and remove the pups (a position I really wanted to avoid). During all my visits with Whisper and her pups, I had intentionally not touched the pups, due to the high energy Whisper radiated around them. If we took the pups out to raise them, how would she react, I wondered; would she become aggressive?

Another day had past when I arrived to visit Whisper and check on the pups under the tree, I was surprised to find her and the pups gone. I stood there looking around for signs of where she may have moved them. The eagle was still sitting in the same tree; three days had passed, and that eagle sat in the same place, on the same branch. I made my way around the upper part of the enclosure and found Whisper had moved her pups up higher on the hill. As I knelt down next to the new tree, I could see Whisper curled up around her pups, just as she should be, and I could see all four tiny little heads bobbing up and down. I got down on my hands and knees and crawled part way in under a large tree branch piled high with snow.

The branch was hanging low to the ground. Freezing snow fell down the back of my jacket ice cold and wet on to my neck, reminding me how much I missed the nice warm cabin. Whisper seemed quiet and not interested in saying hi. I felt satisfied she was keeping the pups warm, and for the time being I decided to head back up to get some other work done inside, where it was warm. Sometime later that day, I had forgotten about the eagle, until I heard the strong flapping of wings above my cabin. I quickly stepped outside and looked up; high above me, the eagle was finally flying off and appeared to be leaving. Two ravens followed close behind, and they seemed to be escorting him off the property. After that evening, there was no sign the eagle had returned.

Eager to make sure the eagle remained gone, I got up early the next day and did my usual check. It continued to be very cold and snowed again, and I hoped the pups did okay on such a freezing night when the wind was howling. Whisper never ceased to confuse me. When I got up to the tree where her pups were, she was off somewhere else. I did not see her when I entered the enclosure, nor did she see me when I walked up the hill as usual. I saw the pile of pups right up next to the trunk, and they seemed motionless. On closer inspection, one of the pups was waking up and moving and beginning to make a little noise.

I sat quietly near the pups, watching them for a moment, waiting for Whisper. I became concerned when it looked like one of the pups was dead. I did not want to crawl under the tree without Whisper present. I remained still and watched as the three other pups moved and bobbed around. Back up at the cabin, two other litters of pups that were born earlier that spring had been hand raised, and whenever one of them woke up, they all woke up. They would search around for mom's warm belly, nipple, and milk.

Something startled me. It was Crazy Horse, who had come up behind me. His ability to walk silently was impressive. I was jealous; I wished I had that ability to walk with that much ease and grace in the wilderness. When he came, I knew Whisper would not be far away. Sure enough, she was right behind him. She lashed out at Crazy Horse, and that distracted her from thinking that I might be up to something. Crazy Horse became caught off-guard as Whisper jumped up on top of him, screaming a low rolling growl; she was full of herself, hackles up and miffed.

Crazy Horse quickly ran back down the hill. With a flash and snow flying, the queen arrived in a flurry.

I was glad I had kept my distance at that moment, and although I did stand up, I remained calm and still. After a brief encounter and a near miss of putting myself in the middle of Whisper's wrath on Crazy Horse. Still all puffed up, Whisper jumped up in my face. In that split-second, Whisper did not seem to recognize the difference between Crazy Horse and me. I thought I might be in trouble. Whisper quickly softened as she greeted me.

She then proceeded to climb over the top of her puppy pile, and as she did, I kept my eye on the motionless pup. Whisper laid her body down, putting her weight on top of the pile. I saw throughout her moving around, the listless pup remained silent and motionless. I thought he was dead. At that time, I left Whisper with her pups, including the motionless one, until I figured out what to do next. After consulting with the other caretakers helping out at the time, it was decided that if the remaining three pups were to survive, we would need to intervene. We would need to join up Whisper's pups with the other pups being hand-raised inside the warm cabin.

I thought that the next time I entered the enclosure, I would pick up the dead pup, which would allow Whisper to focus on her remaining live pups. I was afraid the other pups might meet the same doom from exposure to the elements and not enough mama time, like their lifeless brother. I did not know how Whisper would react if I tried to take all her pups away, so I asked another caretaker to distract her. A few hours later, when I walked back down to the enclosure, I found Whisper with her pups, and to my surprise, the seemingly lifeless pup was alive and moving, bobbing its little head around with the other three pups; they were all making noise at their mother. I was confused but relieved and felt a little embarrassed.

I called out, "The pup is alive!" It felt like a trick had been played on me, or maybe I saw things; I do not know. All I know was I felt at the early of an age five to six days old, the pups were much better off with mama if she would take care of them as they needed in the freezing cold weather. Unfortunately, that was short-lived, as the very next trip to the enclosure, I again saw only three tiny heads bobbing up and down. I got down on my hands and knees and greeted Whisper under the tree branch. I began to talk to her as I got in close enough to see the pups. Three little coal black heads were moving eagerly about her neck, and one coal black pup was sleeping. *That was odd,* I thought; I reached over and scratched Whisper up on her neck, and then for the first time, I reached my hand out and touched the ground near the pups.

No reaction; I did it again, and again, no reaction from Whisper. I reached my hand over the heads of the little ones and gently set my index finger on one tiny little head. I gentle stroked it for a few seconds and then removed my hand. Whisper seemed to care less about my touching the pups. I reached down to touch the motionless pup while Whisper watched. It was cold to my touch. It was dead.

How upsetting! I was ready to greet these little spirits with a big welcome. At that time, I knew it would be best to raise the pups by hand. I reached out and gently picked up the dead pup and set it down again. Whisper picked it up, gently nibbling its head in her teeth and pulling it up close to her body. She licked its little head and neck as if nothing was wrong, and it was still alive. She set it back down on the ground, and I reached out, picked it up, and gently slipped it inside my coat. It was six days old.

While the other caretakers distracted Whisper by feeding her, I quickly and tenderly tucked the three remaining coal black pups inside my jacket. As I walked down the hill with pups in tow, Whisper came running up to me, smelling my jacket where the pups nestled together quietly. I knew she understood I had her pups with me and the people felt that was for the best; she did not show any signs of protest and went back to searching for meat to eat.

A few months later in early fall, we worked again to vasectomize the males, assisting a team of vets who traveled to the sanctuary to perform the procedures. After the surgery, we lost two of the wolves to complications; this included Crazy Horse. The loss of these wolves left a devastating rippling effect on my heart.

Tracy, Zephyr, Whisper, and Crazy Horse.
Photograph courtesy Gary Crandall.

Seasons of the Horse pencil sketch of Majiik
by Tracy Ane Brooks 2014.

PART 2

Seasons of the Horse

CHAPTER 16

My First Horse

Did I die and go to heaven and these horses were here to collect me?

One afternoon in August 1998, I was working at my desk, finishing up an art project, when I decided to take a break. As I left the building, I noticed a lot of activity coming from the wolf enclosures. It was a hot summer day and not typical for the wolves to be so active in the heat. I looked down toward the parking lot hoping to see what all the commotion was about. The trees, thick with summer leaves, made it impossible to see. Normally during this time of the day, the wolves would be sleeping or lounging in the shade. But for some reason, they were all acting restless which made me very curious.

I looked up the hill behind me; all the different packs of wolves were standing at attention, looking at the same thing. I walked down toward the lower buildings, and as I hurried along, I felt like it was taking forever to get down the dirt path leading from my cabin. I walked quickly, looking at the wolves and watching the ground under my feet and the path up ahead of me. Different species of native wild grass had grown thick in the hot summer sun. Browned tips were gently swaying in the warm breeze. As I reached the lower building, I shrugged off the wolf enthusiasm, believing their excitement was no more than a volunteer disrupting something at the meat pad or moving the meat buckets.

The wolves were always eager to eat, no matter what time of day it was (or season of the year). When feeding time arrived, the wolves never missed a beat. And when it came to the meat pad, any movement in that area always captured the attention of every nearby wolf, even in the heat of the day. I quickly forgot the wolves when I looked out toward the parking lot, where arriving visitors parked their cars. To my surprise, two huge black horses were standing next to a truck. I had not seen them come in. The wolves, however, were all eyes.

I remembered these two horses, I had I had seen them before and knew they belonged to a neighbor. I had watched the neighbor riding miles away from the sanctuary. The horses were so stunning, large and shiny, it was hard not to stop and stare at them in awe. My curiosity was piqued and I asked, "Why are they here?" I could not stop staring at the horses as I walked straight out toward them. The horses stood side-by-side, ears pricked, holding their heads up, looking side to side with wide eyes. Like the wolves watching them, the horses were watching the wolves right back. I remember thinking it seemed funny at first glance, two statuesque horses tied to the meat truck, and in a way, it looked as if the horses had been purposefully parked like cars in the lot.

Both horses remained pretty calm and stood a comfortable distance from the wolf enclosures, yet they were very aware of the wolves nearby. Their eyes were wide as they watched me walk up from behind. I saw that neither horse was wearing a saddle on its back. I thought that was pretty cool! How intriguing, the neighbors had ridden across some pretty rough terrain bareback to get here; that must have been challenging. The wolves let out an excited, high-pitched howl as I reached the horses. As if they were yelling at me for some reason.

The howling caused the horses to spin their large bodies around and focus their full attention in the direction I was walking. Their heads were huge, and I could see pink, deep inside their nose; with each heavy breath, their nostrils flared in and out. Short, guttural snorts came from one of them, but both horses were breathing with anxiety. The closer I got, the more amazing the horses looked. I was stunned at how big they were; I had never been so close to such a huge animal. Tall, majestic, I stood in awe at them from ten feet away. I walked to the opposite side of the truck, out of sight from the wolves.

Reluctantly, the horses followed my body; as I looked into their wide eyes, I could see fear and confusion. Why were they here? I was not the only one asking. After a moment, the horses seemed to relax slightly, knowing that it was a person approaching them and not a pack of wolves. I got right up next to one of them, and the horse towered over me. Their large brown eyes were opened wide with concern, and their shiny metallic black coats were lit up by the sunlight. Their long tails reached down and almost touched the ground.

I did not recognize the breed of these majestic giants, but I was struck that this could be a Friesian, the same kind of horse that starred as Goliath in one of my favorite movies, *Ladyhawke.* They sure reminded me of that stunning horse. The horses kept turning and looking in the direction of the wolves, and after a brief scan of the parking lot, they would turn back toward me. They were clearly on edge, and I could not help but wonder if the smells from the meat truck they were tied to had any effect on their fear level.

Did I die and go to heaven and these horses were here to collect me? I pondered the feeling of exhilaration I was experiencing, standing near these larger-than-life creatures. One of the biggest dreams I had as a child was to one day own a horse. Riding the school bus home, I would often daydream that my imaginary horse and I would be outside the window, running alongside the bus. The daydreams seemed more like memories, echoing somewhere beyond my current lifetime. They burned into my mind an image I could never shake, and to this day, those daydreams continue. I often say I would rather ride a horse than drive a car.

I reveled for a few short seconds in pure joy; it felt so natural to be in the presence of horses. In the depth of my heart, I knew there was an empty place that only a horse could fill. If only I could own a horse as magnificent as one of these animals standing right in front of me, well then, that would be beyond my wildest dreams. I became distracted when both horses again quickly turned their heads toward the wolves. I looked over in the same direction and saw Kent walking down the path with the neighbors and their small child. They were getting ready to be on their way. I stopped to say hello and immediately asked about the horses.

I learned that they were semi-retired Percheron workhorses that had spent their lives pulling farm equipment and wheeled carts. Not the same breed as Goliath from the movie, but magnificent regardless. The neighbors were proud of how well the horses were working out for them. The man gently lifted his small son up and set him on the back of one of the horses. I was amazed at how responsive the horse was, even relieved to have a child on his back, some reassurance at the unpredictable wolf sanctuary, perhaps. Here stood two amazing horses with their three amazing people. The horses were so big and yet so gentle that a small child could get on board with only the aid of his father and travel safely across mountainous terrain. This alone impressed me tremendously. My head now reeled with even more questions as the people readied to go, but I did not want to delay them.

I stood there a moment longer, and the neighbor's demeanor shifted to a saddened tone. She then said, "I am afraid I have to sell Moses. My life is changing, and I need to let go of my horse."

Without a moment's hesitation, I interrupted the neighbor and blurted out, "I'll buy him!"

I felt like I was hovering over my own head as I listened to my own voice speak. I surprised myself and looked around, as if I did not know where the outburst originated. I had not given any time to consider the reality of owning a huge horse. Where would I put him? A small wave of panic shot through my veins. A horse was a huge commitment, but for some reason, it felt right, and I could not help think there was no better time than the present moment to fulfill a lifelong dream of owning a horse. For better or worse, I decided to go with my gut.

The neighbor told me that Moses had become uncooperative and seemed to grow worse the older he became. I knew it would not be easy to take on the responsibility of a stubborn old draft horse, but in an odd way, I was very ready to try. I stood there in the parking lot, stunned as I watched the two Percheron horses and their people disappear out of sight. I was thrilled. I had no idea how I was going to do this; we had no corral, no stall, and no pasture fence setup. Not to mention I had not even told Kent yet. But after thinking about it, I could not help but become excited; my life was about to take a new turn. *A most welcomed perk,* I thought.

The more I thought about what I had just gotten myself into, the more I felt it was a smart choice to invest in an older horse. After all, I was not getting any younger myself. I was in my late thirties, perhaps a time when other people might be retiring from owning a horse. Many of the horse people I knew had the fortune to grow up with horses in their lives, a luxury I did not have when I was a kid, but now I could get a horse for my inner child. So in 1998, Moses became the first horse to grace my life: a seventeen-year-old, nearly two thousand pound black Percheron draft gelding. In the twilight of his life, he was over the hill and retired from hard plough work, yet young enough that he would be a great first horse for someone with my experience (or to correctly state, my lack of experience).

We made a good pair, because I too felt I was coming into the twilight years of my life, and I could relate to aging issues on many levels. When I first got to know Moses, he had a worried look in his eye. I wondered what he thought about me; my heart burst at the seams with love for him, but did he feel the same about me? I also had some deep-seated fear after my experience with a feral horse years ago that bucked me off; I nearly broke my back. It took me months to heal, and now I wanted to be safe and gentle with Moses, who outweighed that feral horse by a thousand pounds or better. One of the goals of my owning Moses, at least I hoped, would be that I get over being afraid of riding and learn how to develop a real connection with my horse, a relationship that I felt safe in, experiencing a connection I could learn and evolve.

New dreams and possibilities began to fill my head. I was even thinking about how I could apply what I was learning from Moses to the wolves I was working with in the Ambassador program. I was eager to learn as much as I could about horses. A year after Moses became my first horse, a second horse would follow. Moses had lived with Ikus for some time and knew him well. He was the other horse that visited Mission: Wolf that day my life with horses began. Like Moses, he was a black Percheron gelding; he was a year older than Moses. His name was Ikus; he was more majestic and dominant than Moses, and he seemed like a Viking warrior.

Ikus and Moses were immediate treasures for me, and I became electrified at the thought of working with them. Every cell in my body was energized in the presence of these horses. I recognized this every day. I smiled at the opportunity to care for them, and I knew it would not be easy to do so, but that did not matter. They inspired me to dream big about my future, with them and horse's in general. And now here they were, two beautiful Percheron geldings, full of life and energy. I could hardly believe it. Ikus seemed the perfect addition to my newly formed horse herd.

By the time Ikus came into my life, Moses had grown accustomed to me. Physically, Ikus and Moses looked a lot alike, and they were similar in size too. Moses was nearly all black, and Ikus had one short white sock above his front right foot. Moses had a small star on his forehead, where Ikus had a blaze that went from above his eyes and ended at his pink, velvety soft nose. Moses and Ikus had been teammates many times before, pulling farm equipment through the fields in a nearby town. Moses spurred my interest, and Ikus made me want to learn how to train horses. I developed a passion for learning anything and everything I possibly could about horses.

I remembered seeing the movie *The Horse Whisperer* the first day it came out at theaters, and when I left, I was so inspired. At the time, it had only been a dream to own a horse; reality had yet to present a horse to me. What attracted me to this way of working with horses was the perception that there was a magical or invisible element in connecting to the horse. At least that's what I walked away thinking. After that movie, I spent a lot of time pondering horses and ways of working with them. When Moses finally did arrive in my backyard, I was ready to begin my quest for knowledge. I did not know where this newfound passion would lead me, but I did not let my unclear path discourage me either.

I decided to seek out horse trainers who used positive approaches with their horses. The horse people I seemed to resonate most with believed the study of wild horse behavior was at the foundation of their training methods. Natural horsemanship seemed to be a good place to start. I learned there was no magic involved in the techniques, just a lot of patience and common sense, combined with a unique understanding of horses. From that day forward, I attended as many different horse clinics as I possibly could. It was like starting my life again; I felt honored and thrilled by what I was learning from these amazing horse people. I learned how to be gentle and kind around horses and also establish a lifelong relationship with them.

Watching these incredibly good horse people with their animals was like watching a graceful and beautiful dance, an art form in and of itself. After attending a class or two, I decided that I was not yet ready to learn some of what they were teaching; the information was at a different level than I was, and I did not understand. And other things that I believed I needed to learn, they were not teaching. Although this did not discourage me to discontinue my lessons, what I did decide to do was be more intuitive, like I had been with the wolves. In the lessons I took, the teachers rarely focused on the intuition aspect of the relationship; instead, they put more emphasis on exercises one could do with a horse to achieve specific results. I knew from the relationships I had developed and maintained with the wolves that my intuition was first and foremost.

If I wanted horses to teach me about horse behavior, I picked the perfect two. Moses had some behavioral quirks, but I could learn to work with them. Ikus had no pretenses; he was more of a challenge for me to work with than Moses. Moses let me walk up to him at any time and put a halter on his giant head. Ikus, on the other hand, was a whole different story; he wanted nothing to do with the halter. That was one behavior I hoped to change right away. No matter where Ikus was, if he saw me coming toward him with a halter, even if I were walking out to catch Moses, he would quickly move away. He would even go as far as kicking his heels in the air in front of me.

But the thought of running away from a cookie never occurred to Ikus, and anytime I wanted to walk up to the big horse with nothing but a cookie in hand, he was all over that opportunity. But when it came time to the catch Ikus for a ride, if I did not have a cookie in my hand, and especially if he saw me approach with something resembling a rope hanging from my hand, he became resistant and untrained, acting like a feral horse. It did not seem like the same horse I saw carrying a small child on his back. I did not know him. And I watched him time and time again act up when I went to catch him.

I felt somewhat confused, because I did not quite know how to fix this problem. Nor did I know the root of where the behavior originated from in the first place. I asked myself, was it me? Did I do something wrong to create this problem? I had so much to learn about horses; even so, I thought, *how could I possibly be responsible for Ikus's resistance?* I had only had him for a very short time. So what was happening? Regardless of my inexperience with horses, I knew in my heart that I had the passion for whatever it would take to learn how to fix this.

As a child, on the rare occasion I had the opportunity to ride the neighbor's pony, in order to catch the equine loose in the field, I learned to hide the halter in my jacket and use carrots or other treats as an enticement. This behavior pretty much boiled down to what felt like tricking the pony to catch it. I did not want to resort to food treats if I could help it. To me, it seemed that I was only rewarding the bad behavior by handing out food before the problem reared its ugly head. I wanted to evolve, to stay clear of anything that might reward more bad behavior. Even if I had unwittingly set the pattern, I needed to correct it. I believed I needed to be straight out in all my communications with horses. I did not want to hide anything physical, mental, or emotional from them.

Deep down, I believed that if I kept hiding the halter, it would backfire on me one day. The intention was clear, simple, and basic. All I wanted to do was walk up to Ikus and put a halter on, without a fight or flight.

CHAPTER 17

Outstanding in My Field

My imagination reeled as I thought about mirroring a horse's body language.

I stood outside our small cabin for a few moments, paused, and stared toward the vibrant, green Sangre de Cristo Mountains. It was easy to make excuses and stay inside doing busy work, keeping warm and dry while it poured rain all morning long. The day had a surreal, mystical feel, and now the clouds were moving toward the mountains, and I wanted to get out and feel the sun on my back and work with the horses. My boots crunched the gravel on the wet, rocky dirt. My legs had cramped up earlier, and as I stretched them, I suddenly recognized what I was missing by not being outside in the fresh air. I took a deep breath in through my nose and noticed a sweet, clean smell. The summer had proven to be a wet one, and everything growing was in bloom.

Growing season was short-lived at an elevation of nine thousand feet, yet surprisingly the property had once grown potatoes, turnips, and more. Now that the clouds were passing, it would be a good time to work with Ikus. Being with Moses and Ikus was the most rewarding time of my day. But my inability to walk out and catch Ikus was driving me crazy. It was stressful to work with him when I spent more than half of my time trying to get a halter on the big

148

horse. I wondered what it would be like to walk out to the field and put a halter on Ikus with no fuss.

I scanned across the parking lot as I headed out, looking for the horses. The small field was nearly five acres in size, and the horses could get out of sight behind the barn. Regardless of the moisture, good edible green grass was scarce in the field. We'd have to purchase more precut hay beyond the winter supply to feed out during the hot summer months and compensate for the lack of pasture nutrition. I thought summer was meant for horses to be out to pasture, free grazing on all the high-altitude grass they could find. And it was especially helpful saving a few dollars on hay bales.

The five-acre field was a normal pasture, except there was a lot of overgrowth of rabbit brush and other weeds. These large bushes tended to overpower the little patches of grass struggling to survive. It was prime rabbit brush season, and the bushes were in full bloom. Tiny yellow flowers budded at the tips of its gray-green branches. The storm had left branches bent and broken, and what seemed like hundreds of little yellow buds lay scattered in the mud. The sun's rays beat down hot, like nature's version of aromatherapy, releasing the fragrances of the field. The scent of the rabbit brush dominated the air, its pungent turpentine odor nearly smothered out the bouquet of other wonderful, earthy fragrances.

Rabbit brush smelled nothing like the antiseptic stems and leaves of the sagebrush. I often mistook the rabbit brush for sagebrush, usually because of its size, shape, and especially sage green colored leaves with gray stems. But as I got to know the difference, I saw that most of the rabbit brush around the pasture was a grass green color, more vivid than the soft color of sage. The five-acre pasture looked more like an overgrazed weed field than any green foliage the horses would normally choose to eat. The sky lit up as the last of the storm's ominous, blue-black clouds vanished over the Sangre mountaintops, and a gentle gust of wind brushed past me. I could hear it as it swept through the valley behind me. All around, the atmosphere was renewed.

For a day that started out surreal and ominous, it was now vibrant, refreshed, and full of life. Birds were chirping in the trees; how I loved being outside. Joy filled my heart and senses as I walked in nature; I compared that feeling to standing in a space between time and nature. An electric silence took over my being, and for a second, I felt I was where bliss and connection collided to become one.

I had good traction on the soles of my boots and could walk at a rapid pace through the muddy terrain. The tops of my boots became soaked before I reached the barn. It was a good thing I had already planned to work in the mud. I stopped at the barn and walked inside, where I kept the horses' tack. I gathered one of the newly purchased draft horse halters and proceeded to where I believed the horses to be. A feeling of exhilaration came up in me as if I had been out dancing in the pouring rain. I was excited that I might have a new idea about how to potentially cure Ikus of running from me. I unclipped the chain of the large entry gate and swung it open.

I had to think about carrying the burgundy-colored nylon halter openly in my hand and avoided the temptation to slip it into my shirt. I had been hiding the halter from Ikus but now bounced it as if to announce its approach in a carefree manner. I remember feeling nervous about the idea I had; still, I tried to bluff my way past and continue to bang the halter against my leg as I walked. I became quiet long enough to slip my body in between the two heavy gates inside the five-acre field. I could see the horses off in a secluded corner, coincidently as far away from the gate as they could be. Their heads lowered as they grazed, and they did not seem to notice I had just come through the gate and was walking toward them.

The field spread out behind the back of the horse barn and was the horses' primary living space. I felt pretentious and weird walking across the field, as if I was intentionally trying to attract attention to myself. What was I doing? Normally, I would approach the horses in a calm and quiet manner, but today was different. I ignored the judgmental thoughts I was having about my abilities—or rather inabilities—with the horses (or at least attempted to) and continued my walk to find them. I made no attempt to hide the huge halter, as I had in the past.

I had made up my mind that I would figure out some way to communicate with Ikus at the level I desired to, to gain his trust and respect so he would not run from me. I had been thinking that if I modified my behavior and body language to be more like Ikus's behavior, he might better understand my intention. I wanted to mirror the horse's behavior in a similar way that horses mirrored one another, only modified as a human, and if this worked, these ideas may even work with the wolves too. I was not sure where it would take me, but I was willing to try and excited to see what would happen. I thought a lot about how I could approach Ikus (or any other resistant, feral or fearful horse, for that matter) and consistently get respect and trust. My dream was for my life with horses to be rewarding, reasonably smooth, often easy, and tremendously joyful.

This was especially important as I grew older and needed to take care of myself for my long-term well-being, which began to override my desire to act like a daredevil.

I wanted to follow what felt good to my heart, and many of the training methods I was learning went against the free-flowing, intuitive, instinctual relationship I desired with the animals in my life. I was beginning to believe the best way to go about trying something new was to throw away everything I had previously learned about working with horses, to evolve my behavior and use the body language I was learning in ways I'd never thought of doing with a horse before. An ultimate goal would be for me to have a thought or a mental picture flash through my head and have the horse respond. This visualization would be one of the intentions that I wanted from my horse. The reward would be the horse reacting in the proper way, making my thought a solid reality. I had a long way to go.

In order for this big dream to work the way I planned, I knew I needed to work hard and to be patient. I learned I would spend a good amount of time fumbling until I could figure out what I was seeking. Horses had only been in my life a short time, but they were like the wolves in the way that my thoughts were not off-limits to them. For better or worse, I was being read like a book, by the wolves and now by the horses too; that meant I had to step it up and learn how to read the wolves and horses right back. The horses' body language and the energy that surrounded them motivated me to become keen to horse language. I believed this would help me become a better person and somehow work stronger and be more confident with the wolves.

During this same time, I happened to see a video documentary about a horseman who rode after a feral mustang. The feral horse had never worn a halter, and I was intrigued by the horseman's goal: to catch, train, and ride the horse in a short time, using methods he developed watching wild horse behavior as a young man. The video was inspiring and indeed unique. I did not know a lot about traditional horse training methods, but I believed this was different somehow. For me, the most important part was when I saw the horseman's horse mirror the feral mustang. I recognized that both horses mirrored one another to some degree, and that fascinated me beyond description.

And the way my mind often works, I learn things backwards; maybe I am dyslexic, even though I have never been formally diagnosed. If I am interested in something, I have to watch it repeatedly to understand it. I often misunderstand anything I watch or hear only once. And this made it challenging for me to study other horse people's work. I could not remember much of what the man talked about from the video; I was distracted by what the horses were doing.

I think I may have walked away from that video with little different picture in my head than it was intended to demonstrate. Needless to say, I aspired to mirror the horse. I was not sure exactly what I was inspired to do, but I thought it would be smart to take my time and stay safe. Most importantly, I needed to keep the horse safe, too (and, fingers crossed, sane with their recently acquired, inexperienced owner). I desired to see from the horse's perspective what they saw in me as I approached Ikus with a halter in my hand. The wolves taught me to listen well.

I wanted to stand in Ikus's hooves, so to speak, to look out from his giant brown eyes and see the real me, and then face the changes I needed to make in order to overcome his resistance. I thought about how wild horses used mimicry or mirroring to learn from one another and survive. I wondered ... would it be possible for me to mimic wild horse behavior?

It was hard to believe at his age, that Ikus still had the get-up-and-go of a young horse, and he often caused quite a dramatic fuss. I did not know what fueled his resistance to being captured; horse language was foreign to me. Was his behavior a learned behavior, or was he evasive out of fear? He may have had a bad experience in the past, or maybe he did not like me.

Or was his behavior a form of defiance, displayed for the benefit of the other horses as a lead horse? Perhaps as the dominant gelding, in some way being captured was a sign of weakness in the eye of the herd. Most of all, I wondered whether the horses behavior was a reflection of something in me; could I figure out what?

I am certain there were other ways of solving his behavior. But it occurred to me to mirror horse behavior in a modified, two-legged way. My imagination reeled as I thought about the reality of what Ikus's body language was silently trying to communicate to me. I wanted to know. A strange but optimistic feeling came up in my gut, and I felt encouragement coming in from somewhere and being downloaded into my being. Even though I was working alone, and nobody else was there, I could feel energy for somewhere else. I could not resist following these promptings. Whether I was on the right track with mirroring or not, at least I was at a starting point that felt right to me.

One of the first things I wanted to understand was my approach to Ikus, rather what he physically saw as I walked toward him with a halter. There was something he saw that caused him to distrust and feel the need to flee. Could he somehow see the apprehension I was feeling toward my failures to catch him previously or my nervousness about future attempts?

I could think of a million reasons why Ikus wanted to run from me and could speculate to the end of this book and still never know the exact reason behind this behavior. I did not blame Ikus for this behavior; how could I? When I first started to take care of him, I'd used carrots or cookies to get his attention. I believed I spent the previous months tricking him into allowing me to catch him.

Without meaning to, I reinforced Ikus's resistant behavior. At first, it became impossible to catch him without treats. And not long following, it became difficult even with the use of treats. In fact, there was no guarantee that I would catch him at all. In plain and simple terms, I realized I'd been rewarding Ikus all along for being a problem catch. At the time, I had already had more than a decade of working with the wolves in public, and I'd experienced similar behavioral problems working with them.

I remember how it felt working with Shaman in public. I had become far too familiar with, and often downright frustrated by, the Ambassador wolves running away from me when I needed to catch and leash them. On the rare occasion we were temporarily gifted private use of an enclosed tennis court or a secured school courtyard for exercise, Shaman would become mischievous, like a little pixie. Letting him loose into new digs was stressful. To catch the playful, feral and free running pixie wolf after he had a taste exploring new territory, took more patience than we had time for during school hours. I dreaded letting him loose into a new environment.

It was especially difficult to catch Shaman in front of an audience of people. All he wanted to do was explore, romp, and take in all the new smells. When the time came to leash up, Shaman could feel the uncomfortable energy rising up in me. His behavior seemed to magnify, and his wildness was enhanced if people were laughing at the situation. I would become embarrassed by my lack of control to help catch this elusive pixie.

Watching pixie wolf run away from Kent, darting in and around, being a general smarty-pants, was discouraging. In order to catch Shaman, it had to be on his own time, not on any school's schedule. What concerned me was "pixie time" did not take into consideration the school bell ringing, followed by eight hundred kids of all ages pouring into the halls. When exercise time finished, we wanted to get back to the wolf van, loaded and ready to leave, not twiddling our thumbs, trying to figure out what to do next in order to get the wolf back on the leash. In the end, Kent was the one to catch Shaman using play or a food treat, and I would do my best to go with it. It was a good insight into the nature of the wolf.

I had faced exactly the same problem with Shaman and other wolves up until that point, and ironically, I had used the same way of dealing with the problem again and again. Only, instead of cookies or carrots, it was hot dogs and kielbasa sausage for Shaman. Thankfully, I had all the time in the world to work with Ikus; no stress due to time constraints imposed by strict school schedules or the pressure of public appearances. On several occasions during my time outstanding in the field with Ikus, I would receive strong impressions, that if I could resolve the catch problem with this horse, I could do the same with the wolves.

A squeaky wet boot noise had developed as I walked through the field. "Squeak, squeak, squeak," the sound seemed to go with the beat of my step. I approached the horses with two different noises going at the same time. I kept the halter jingling loudly against my leg, and with my boot squeak, squeaking away, the horses immediately took notice. They were standing in mud too, but looked statuesque, eyes wide and heads held high, with their ears pricked in my direction, alert and curious. Horses responded in a similar way living wild as they did in domestic situations when they assessed any potential threat approaching. They would stop grazing, raise their heads, and start evaluating if they were in any potential danger.

The more experience I gained working with horses, the more I recognized deep down wolves, horses, and humans were all one and the same. I called out to Ikus, as I got closer, and the horses seemed to relax, recognizing my voice from a distance. I could see their body language softened ever so slightly. Their heads lowered, but they did not go back to grazing; they continued to stand and watch me walking toward them, grass hanging from Moses lower lip. They seemed to notice I was louder than normal, and they all looked at me with concern in their long faces. The rain had soaked the ground just enough to give it a muddy, slippery surface. Many times, the horses would run up toward me and come to a sliding stop in the mud right in front of me. This did not stop the concern I was feeling about the horses running hard in the mud, and I wanted to avoid that.

I did not want Ikus to become scared of the halter noises as I approached, and take off like a wild banshee and slide into the fence or do something that caused him (or another horse) to get injured. But I knew once I was close enough for him to recognize what I was up to, he would flee. By the time I got around thirty yards away from the horses, I had worked out a plan in my mind. I wanted to make whatever I was about to do a light-hearted experience and maybe even fun. A game of sorts, even creating some ground rules (although I did not know what the rules were yet).

I believed that once I learned the rules, the game would be over. Problem solved. Ikus represented years of animals that ran away from me, although they were canines; still, this was a way I could face the problem head on, thanks to the horse. Obviously, Ikus would make his own rules as we went along. Or have no rules at all, so in essence he would be the one in charge of the game. It would be up to me to learn how to follow his lead and interpret those rules. Ikus begin to raise his head as I continued to approach him with the halter swinging out in front of me.

I had hoped he would let me walk right up to him. Moses stood there, curious, as I reached him, ready for a greeting. But as I went right up to Moses, Ikus took off running, and Moses did too, briefly turning his head back toward me as if to question what was the big deal and why did he have to run? Moses naturally and without question mirrored Ikus's behavior. In horse herd mentality, when the leader reacts, the others respond accordingly and follow. Off they went in a flash, their heads flipped up and ears pricked forward in the opposite direction, away from me. Heels kicked the air as bits and pieces of wet mud were flung in my direction. I stood and watched as the horses gained speed across the five-acre field.

Horses, like wolves, have keen vision, and I learned that even if Ikus was clear across the five-acre field, and at a distance, he could still see my every move and understand my body language. That made sense to me. In the wild, they would be watching each other's posturing or body language from great distances. To test and see if the horses could read my body language as easily as they could read each other's at a distance, I decided to run out immediately after they all took off. The horses turned and came to a stop in the opposite corner of the field; simultaneously, I turned with them and stopped too. They looked at me with wide eyes that seemed to be saying, "What are you doing?"

I kept the halter in plain sight, and I continued bouncing it off my leg as I stood watching the horses watch me. Ikus's head was up in the air, the highest of all the horses, and I could see his nostrils snort warning noises in my direction. The others looked at me questioningly, wondering what Ikus was huffing about. I waited for a moment and watched their bodies. When they seemed to relax, I again walked toward them. It took me several moments to get across the field, and when I did, Moses just stood there and let me walk right up to him. I walked by him and stroked him gently on the neck. Ikus was standing beyond Moses, and when he saw me pass around Moses's body, he again bolted off back across the field to where he started.

This time, I was able to run off with Ikus and not involve Moses or the other horse. Moses started to follow Ikus, but then he stopped halfway across the field. Moses seemed to recognize that I was only focused on Ikus. It was interesting how quickly Moses figured that out; he suddenly realized that I was putting no pressure on him whatsoever. The only pressure that was coming towards him was when he ran with Ikus. Once Moses figured out that he could stand, the other horse did, too. I gently jogged along the center of the field, putting my energy on Ikus as he swung a wide circle to the other side of the five-acre field and again headed back toward the safety of the herd. I turned, but he had already made his way past me. He moved quickly around one of the other horses and stopped.

Ikus was out of sight for a second, so I decided to stop and wait. He paused as if he were hiding or pretending to be invisible. I stood for a moment and then began to walk toward him again. As I reached the horse Ikus was hiding behind, that horse froze, holding his head high and keeping his eyes wide. I could see the animal was on the edge of bolting from my approach and being caught between the two of us. For him, the pressure was high enough; he nearly took off from the anxiety alone. After I brushed right past him, holding my focus on Ikus the whole time, the horse sighed in relief and dropped his head down.

I noticed the horse relax when I faced away from him and did not look directly at him. But if I shifted my focus back to him, turned my eyes or upper body in his direction, his attitude would tense up, and he would flash me a brief stare, just prior to bolting. I felt that he probably perceived me as a predator. I recognized how tense and nervous I was too when I caused the other horse to move. I reminded myself to take a deep breath and let it out. Ikus's demeanor changed when he saw me coming around the backside of the big red horse. I wanted him to see that I intended to catch him; in fact, I wanted him to see that I was determined to befriend him.

Moses stood watching me with his lower lip hanging down, surprised at my new approach to Ikus, and he seemed to have questions in his eyes. He was smart, and he knew what I wanted. As Ikus again made his way past Moses, this time he threw out a couple of protest hops as he ran by. Moses remained as still as a statue. I had only planned to work for a short time on the first day. Ikus was already working hard to stay away from me as I again made my way back across the field. I could see this was going to be a long process. I did not want to push Ikus, and I needed to think about the meanings of the day's events. I took in air and held a deep breath.

As I did, I became aware that one of my hands was tucked tightly in my pants pocket. I removed it and dropped my hand and arm loosely at my side. When I did this, Ikus reacted. He stopped running like a mad man, turned, and looked curiously at me, softening ever so slightly. In response to his change, I immediately stopped and took a step backwards, offering the horse a release from the pressure of the halter. I realized how I could use my body as a pressure release tool and reward the horses from a distance. Ikus stopped and faced me; his head was slightly lower when he did. He was breathing quietly and not blowing out loud warning snorts. I was a distance away from him, but when I watched the big horse relax, I decided that was good enough for me to stop that day. I felt exhilarated at achieving a brief communication with this stubborn horse.

Instead of walking away from Ikus as his heels brushed past my head, as I had in the past, I left him standing in the mud, facing me. Come to think of it, that might have been one of the first times he had focused on me. I walked away satisfied and feeling like even though I did not get the halter on him, I achieved something that day. That was the clearest body language I had seen him display toward me since I'd had him. On some level, I connected with Ikus. I could not wait to head back out to the five-acre field the next day. I was going to continue to mirror Ikus, holding the halter in my hand. The ground had dried out over night and was much easier to walk across, so I thought maybe we would work a little longer that day.

I planned to use my body language to put a little more pressure on Ikus when he ran and acted out toward my intent to put the halter on him. And when he became soft, I would become soft; when he stopped and faced me, I would back off of him and give him a break. I walked out to the barn and grabbed the halter again. The horses were in the same area they were the previous day. As I approached, Moses did not even bother to move. I noticed immediately as I got closer to Ikus that he had a slightly better attitude. I wasn't alarmed that the horses might have an accident due to poor footing, and I had more confidence than the previous day. I knew what to expect and how to act; now, I just needed to practice and refine my new art.

I wanted to understand what Ikus was feeling more than anything. What was going on in the big Percheron's mind when I mirrored him? Was he scared or confused or resentful? At first, he was hard to read. I tried to stand in his hooves and see what I could learn from him that day. I tried to pay more attention to my body language and the signals I was giving out. I remembered how Ikus reacted to my hands in my pockets, so I worked on keeping my hands out of my pockets. That was tougher than I thought it would be. I played around with my hands in my pockets around the wolves too. And I noticed that when I had my hands in my pockets, the horses and wolves would react a little different, more apprehensive than if I approached them with hands out and arms relaxed, loosely at my sides.

I avoided bending over or crouching down like how a predator stalking a horse might do. I worked at walking or running in a neutral way, keeping my hands at my sides and my spine upright in a confident yet nonthreatening way. The more we moved around the five-acre field, the more I learned that my body movements had an important influence on the direction Ikus moved. If I held my left arm out, it would send him off to the right. If I held my right arm out, then off to the left he would go in the big field. If I hurried my energy and movement up, he would respond and take off faster. If

I slowed my energy and movement down, he would slow; we were already making quite a connection.

I saw clearly how my intent to catch him was so strong it created resistance that would come back to spike me and cause me to have to start over. Any noise or visual invitation I gave him to wear the halter would cause him to flee. Out of sight, out of mind. What I found amusing was Ikus genuinely seemed to believe that if he could not see me, then I did not see him. To his surprise, he discovered that I could see him, even if he had gone as far as to hide behind the horse trailer. When I rounded the corner behind him, he acted surprised, and his body language went into defensive mode, I was beginning to feel it had little to do with fear of me.

His defiance had more to do with someone or something else trying to manage his time—his free will. He just wanted to graze and not be pulled from his horse world to participate in the human world. Midway through our session that day, Ikus was telling me something by moving off and away from me sooner than he had the previous day.

He took off running across the field, clearly letting me know that he had grown even more sensitive to what I was doing than he'd been. His personal space had broadened, and now all of a sudden, he only felt safe on the opposite side of the field, as far away from me as he could get. Even though I had been a long-distance runner for many years, going back and forth across the five-acre field was tiring. It was a challenge to focus one eye on the ground where I was about to step.

As Ikus began his descent yet again, he purposefully veered off in the direction of Moses and Raven, as if to say, "If I have to move, then everyone moves now." He scattered the other horses like balls in a game of pool.

Ultimately, I believed that if I approached Ikus in a neutral way, it would help me convince him I was worthy of his trust. My intuition helped keep me focused and allowed me to move freely with him. My peripheral vision helped me see subtle signals that the horses were giving out when I was not looking directly at them. Ikus behaved worse as I mirrored him that day, and I thought I must look like a fool, running around with this horse. Was I really doing the right thing? He seemed more fearful of me.

Ikus kept his eye on me from a much greater distance and reacted to my approach faster, with lots of aerial displays, throwing his hindquarters up in the air, jumping, and kicking up his heels. I was glad for the distance between us. However, I still don't believe that fear had anything to do with his behavior that day. He was acting like a spoiled, snotty brat. I was certain that if he'd had hands, he would have flipped me the bird and done so more than once (or at least stuck his fingers in his ears, waving them as he made faces at me while he threw his tantrum, heels in the air).

It seemed he was defiant this time, defensive and retaliatory, kicking out at me from a distance like a bucking bronco with a bone to pick. I could hardly believe this was the same docile, submissive, well-trained horse I'd seen harnessed up to pull a plough or carrying that young boy. Ikus ran from me, spurring me to keep running too. I didn't pretend that I could keep up with him, much less try to chase him. It wasn't like that at all. To mirror him meant more like running with him, parallel. I lined my hips up to his front shoulders, which seemed to capture his attention the most. If I fell back toward his hindquarters, where horses drove other horses from, my intent at a connection would temporarily become lost, replaced with a different understanding by the horse, and that was to "move!"

Standing or moving to the hindquarters of the horse was a valuable place for a lesson, but not for mirroring horse behavior. Driving a horse is a whole different story. I worked hard to keep my hips aligned with Ikus's shoulders, even at a distance from across the field. We did lots of circling around the five-acre field, and if he got too far ahead, I tried not to let it stress me out and simply realigned myself and started over. Moses and the other horses did very well to not become involved, in spite of Ikus attempting several times to run up and hide behind them, or use them as decoys.

Sometimes it looked like Ikus was hoping to displace my energy and attention onto the other horses. Near the end of the second day, I begin to compare what I was doing with Ikus to a dance of sorts, a dance of communication. My goal for that day was the same as the day before. Once, Ikus stopped running and let me approach him with the halter in hand I would be done. And as long as he stayed facing me for a few seconds, I would back off and give him a reward through the release of my body. We continued our mirror dance until he finally stopped. A few moments later, his sudden stop caught me off-guard, and I missed stopping at the same time as he did.

I ended up taking a few steps forward, out of place. In turn, this made him jump forward, confused and worried I was coming in to get him. He went forward, rethinking his situation. Once he stopped again, I recognized the importance of good timing and synchronicity with his rhythm. If I did not get the timing just right, it would push him off away from me, confuse the heck out of him, and make him run again. When he paused and stood quiet, I would pause for a moment and then take a few steps calmly in his direction.

Without looking directly at him, I began sidestepping toward him. I wanted Ikus to feel relaxed when I relaxed, and that was not happening. Thanks to the wolves, I was very familiar with sidestepping up to feral or shy animals, and I had learned that my eyes alone were cause enough for these sensitive beings to become unsettled and move away from me. The whole looking-away thing was a valuable lesson for me in how powerful a stare could be and how confusing it could be to another animal. I also learned how a simple look could create movement in an animal. Before this day, I did not recognize the depth of distrust this horse had toward me.

Why should Ikus trust me? I was reasonably new to him, and I understood how much it meant to take time to get to know someone and develop a relationship of trust. Those relationships built on time were better, lasted longer, and felt more comfortable. It made perfect sense to me that horses could be the same with trust issues as people were. I looked at Ikus's eyes, without thinking; I caught myself but it was too late. That was all it took to spur him into another run-off session. Back across the field we went. We'd been at this for a good twenty minutes by now, and I was growing tired.

I stepped along beside him at a distance of forty yards or better, and this time he stopped. He spun his rear around, pointing away from me, and brought his face forward, toward me. He was getting closer and closer as the moments passed. I felt he was growing more comfortable with my presence, or rather the halter swinging around. He still held his head high and kept his eyes open wide. I stopped too and looked down at his feet; my timing had improved significantly since I had begun this mirroring work.

I was becoming tuned in to him and could see that he noticed this subtle reaction I had to his movement and was at a distance, studying it, studying me.

When he took a couple of steps toward me, it surprised me. I was not prepared for him to step toward me, even if it was at a distance; he still made a step in my direction. I took this as a signal that he was at least thinking about me. I responded immediately and took a couple of steps backwards, away from him, using my body as a release. As much as I physically could, I wanted to bridge the gap of communication with this horse through the use of my body as a release tool.

My brief image of perfection burst as he suddenly changed back to Viking Ikus. He snorted and kicked up dirt as he dug his heels deep into the ground; it seemed to be a repeating theme for him to kick dirt out behind him at me as he took off in a full run. In a way, he used that behavior to challenge my intentions. Without hesitation, I took off in a full run, too. Well, the human version of a run, in comparison to a horse. Fortunately for me, the long-distance runner was still within me, and I was in good enough shape to achieve short but controlled bursts of speed.

Once I was running, I found that if I kept my body as parallel to him as humanly possible and corrected myself when I fell out of sync he began to understand what I wanted. Still he remained too reluctant to give it to me. I kept my hips and shoulders lined up as best I could as we both neared a quarter of the way around the field in a circle again, he gave in and turned to face me, stopping all movement. I did not have time to stop and reward him, and before I could respond, Ikus turned quickly away from me and ran back in the other direction. After two more short rounds in the five-acre field, I caught back up with him. This time, I immediately lined up with his shoulders. I felt a little energetic spark or charge from this exact mirroring moment, and I noticed how quickly Ikus came to a stop. When he stopped, I immediately came to a stop. It seemed by sheer accident, I caught his timing and movement just right.

It startled me when he let out a loud snorting noise. I jumped up slightly, caught myself and took a deep breath in, and released it. This time, he stopped the closest he had so far in all the work we had done that day. He seemed to release tension through his breath too, like I had. He lowered his head and neck and gave a little shake. I refrained from looking directly at him. Instead, I looked at his feet and watched his head with my peripheral vision. Right then, I had to retrain myself about the significance of eye contact when working with an animal to develop trust and a long-term relationship. I looked at his body and not his face. I could see his ears pointing in my direction; that seemed like a good sign. I felt hopeful that Ikus obviously heard the breath I let out and was doing a little lick and chew, as a sign of submission and acceptance.

I could not help but notice that his body language was a little more relaxed. He stretched his neck out and let out a small yawn, and I thought this would be a great place to stop for the day. What more could I ask for? He was facing me, relaxed, with a lowered head and soft eyes. We'd been working for less than an hour, and I could not help feeling concerned that despite my good efforts, I wasn't getting as far and as fast as I hoped. I felt impatient. I wanted results that day, but instead I walked inside and hung up the halter, another day unworn. I had to encourage myself to keep trying; I was not quite sure about my mirroring experiment, yet I felt driven to keep going.

Two things could happen: one, he would stop running from me altogether and allow me to halter him, or two, I would never catch him again, and he would never trust me after that. Number one was my obvious choice, and I could not even think of losing what little trust I did have, or making him more fearful of me. Having doubts about my little mirror experiment was natural, at least that's what I told myself as I mentally retraced the previous day's journey. I hadn't been able to get the halter anywhere near Ikus. And it seemed as though I'd lost ground instead of moving forward. I was frustrated despite managing to end the day on a good note.

On the second day, I began to focus on my demeanor. I asked myself whether my energy was too much like that of a predator, and I considered how I could change and soften my approach. But that day, my timing was off, and Ikus's behavior was challenging, to say the least. I had tried to match my movements to his, but it was clearly learning through the experience process.

On the third day, Ikus had yet another lesson for me to learn, one that I would not have imagined, and once again, it would leave me confused and doubtful. When I entered the five-acre field that day, he let me walk right up to him. That shocked and thrilled me; I stopped about twenty feet away, not sure what to think. I held out the halter, and he showed no reaction to it whatsoever. I walked right up to him, reached out, and put a rope around his neck.

Wow! I'd caught him right off the bat. Maybe my gut feeling was right: mirroring a hard-to-catch horse seemed to work, even though the day prior it had not. I slipped the halter around his nose and up one side of his face, then back down the other and hooked the clasp. That was too easy. Feeling victorious, I turned excitedly and began to walk him back toward the barn, when instantly his energy shifted.

He turned away from me with such force that it yanked the lead rope out of my hand. Off he went, bucking and kicking across the field at full speed, the lead rope dancing in the wind behind him. Once again, I was caught off-guard. I just stood there in disbelief, trying to figure out what to do next. Did I just throw the last few days of work out the door? Clear across the field he went, and then he stopped and looked at me, reading my reaction. I very much felt like a fool; he seemed to be flipping me the bird, with his energy and attitude.

I decided to do just what I had done before. It was too late for me to take off running, so I calmly started walking toward him. Ikus turned away from me and took off in a full run. This time, he ran behind an old brown horse trailer that had been placed in the five-acre as a wind block and to trailer-train the horses. He stopped behind it, disappearing momentarily from sight. Feeling tricked and defeated, it took me a few minutes to get my two-legged body over to the trailer. Once I moved around to the side of the trailer, I could tell he thought I could not see him. It was as if we were playing hide-and-seek, and I was it.

He was so into the illusion that he was hidden behind the horse trailer, it seemed that he was already off thinking about something else and had completely forgotten about me. I could see him clear as day; his back was to me, and when I reappeared into his line of sight, he seemed stunned. His face showed surprise as if he were a person; I found that quite comical. Until he saw me, I believe he thought I had truly vanished or that I had no clue where to find him because his hiding place was just that good. I laughed at him, and his head shot up and off he sprang, like a deer escaping from a lion, halter lead dragging at his side. I had to remind myself that I did not want to appear like a predator, even though it was easy to do.

I wanted to pique his natural curiosity by mirroring his behavior in a neutral way. And I needed to get hold of him, because he might get tangled in that loose lead rope. Being a reasonably new horse owner, I worried a lot because I did not have enough experience or confidence in the outcome of my training. As he took off from behind the horse trailer, I was just getting warmed up. I felt my intent reach out and connect with him; I hooked my body into his movement. I intentionally slowed my body movements, and he instantly reacted by slowing his movements. For a split-second, he mirrored me! *What?*

I could not believe it. I had not even thought of that possibility; this behavior excited me to no end. I didn't understand why Ikus had allowed me to put the halter on him that day, but now that he had it on, I slowed my pace down to a walk, and it made me smile to see that even halfway across the field, Ikus also slowed to a walk. I kept walking forward and waited until he turned to face me and stood still; then I changed my direction to face Moses, who was standing right there within arm's reach. I gently reached out my hand as I walked by and began to stroke Moses on the side of his face, and I talked to him, telling him what a good boy he was. I thanked him for not running from me or adding to Ikus's fear of being caught.

Ignoring Ikus gave him the freedom to walk up and stand right behind me. I saw the lead rope motionless on the ground as he stood looking at me, giving Moses attention and contemplating my next move. I gently moved over and stepped down on the rope. I felt a little tug—not enough to pull the lead out from under my boot, but just enough for Ikus to pull and recognize he was caught and give up, which he did. Moses had taken an interest and began sniffing the halter on Ikus's head. I reached over to Ikus and gently stroked his neck too, verbally reassuring him while he investigated Moses's reaction (or lack of reaction) to the halter. I though this would be a great place to end the third day.

On the fourth day, Ikus was back to his need for distance. I could get no closer than twenty-five yards to him. I worked with him for around an hour, which was about the right amount of time. I felt it was both physically and mentally challenging enough for us both.

I dedicated myself to doing at least an hour each day, regardless of the results, always ending on a positive, relaxed note. It was a little cooler the fourth day, and I wasn't sure whether the change was because of the weather or because he was just feeling spunky. Either way, he was in the air and ran away from the halter (and me) in no time. I stood there in a daze. He'd caught me off-guard with his speedy reaction, and I hesitated until I remembered what I was there to do. Then I took off running in a direction parallel to him.

He made it across the five-acre field and ran around behind the horse trailer again. I laughed out loud when I saw this; he must have remembered this brief evasive measure and now wanted to repeat it. To him, out of sight was out of mind. Clearly, he believed I was not coming and stopped, relaxing when he could not see me. Again to his surprise, I appeared from around the trailer. But this time, I faced away from him as I walked. I was trying to keep my energy moving forward, not in a predatory or threatening way, rather calmly and confidently, like a matriarch mare might.

He hesitated for a second as he thought about this, and then he began walking away. But he was walking, not bolting. Even so, he was still giving off rigid body language. He gave me clear, silent signals he was not going to cooperate anytime soon. I learned early on studying horse training if you start a lesson with a horse, it was very important to finish it and do so on a positive note; you can't just up and walk away in the middle of a lesson. The consequence of doing that would be a confused horse, and the next lesson would be that much more challenging.

The reason I thought about that was because I recognized I had not had anything to drink when I got out of bed that morning. And I had forgotten to bring water outside to drink; I was thirsty and was tempted to stop, leave the field, and go get a drink of water, but I refrained. It was tough for me to focus my attention back to Ikus that day. Doing the work the way I wanted was going to take time and patience. I was not sure I had it in me to make a real connection with Ikus. I sincerely hoped I could but found myself wanting to become distracted. I had a feeling in my gut telling me the day would be challenging.

I was using an unorthodox manner to resolve this problem. My behavior probably made me look like a crazy lady, but if I could catch Ikus after four days of working one hour a day, mirroring his behavior, that would be great by me and well worth it. In reality, I had no idea how long it was going to take to achieve my dream of a stress free catch (or even if it would work; there were no guarantees that this gentle experiment would succeed). There were brief moments of encouragement that kept me going. I felt I was connecting to Ikus quicker; I had already out run into the field and started to dance with him. After a few moments, it became easier as I began to warm up and move in sync with the horse; I noticed him paying much more attention to me. It was like he was looking at me, thinking about me. I had been showing Ikus behaviors he'd never seen from a human before, and I could tell this made him look at me in a whole new way.

He still needed time to trust me and respect me as a leader. Days went by, and not much seemed to change. Ikus continued to resist my attempts to mirror him and stop him from running away from me. I'd been so sure that body language was the key to communication, but now I was beginning to question whether this was going to work at all. The fear that my intuition was letting me down began to gnaw at me; if I could not trust my inner promptings, then who on earth could I trust? There was just a little spark of drive that was telling me I couldn't give up yet, to keep trying just for a few more days. It seemed natural that I ask myself if my attitude causing this resistance from Ikus.

A breakthrough finally came at around the twelve-day mark. I walked out into the field, halter in hand, feeling more confident than I had in days. The dance between Ikus and me was shaping up, and I was feeling moments of true connection. And I liked it. I began to feel a newfound confidence in my intuition and appreciation for my open heart with animals. After two weeks, I knew what to do, how to use my body, and how to approach Ikus, and the timing of my movements was improving. Most importantly, I knew that the message I was trying to send through my body and energy was becoming much clearer to the horse; he was reading my intentions and understanding. That day, he did not run away; in fact, he moved toward me when he saw me coming, even with the halter in hand.

I walked right up to him and easily put the halter on. I jumped for joy in my mind and made sure to give him lots of praise, happy talk, and affection. He had just given me a great gift. This mighty Percheron had taught me more about myself than I could have imagined. From that moment on, this experience shaped the way I approached all the animals in my life. I was learning to identify and understand the small, subtle messages I had been sending him in my body language and the way I felt about myself. I learned how he perceived many things about me, and on different levels, too.

Physically, it took me a few times of working with Ikus to figure out that approaching the horses with my hands in my pockets caused a certain reaction. If I were slouching, bent over, or hunched forward, I would get a fearful prey reaction. Ikus would immediately flee, as if I were a predator. When he watched me coming toward him, I knew he could see how I felt by the way I carried myself. I believed he saw someone who was unsure of their approach, and he was right. I had little experience working with horses prior to Moses, and I had no confidence when I started to work with them. After all, Ikus and Moses were two-thousand-pound draft horses, and I was used to handling one-hundred-pound wolves. Handling the drafts made handling the wolves seem easy, even though it was not. Horses were a different kind of creature, but I could relate to the vulnerable prey side of their nature.

Ikus was especially alert as I mirrored his movements, and these were the most endearing, fascinating moments to me. In that mirror time, I felt a real connection. It was as if I had briefly stepped through a doorway into understanding and evolving animal communications. And in that brief moment, two become one, and the universe was in perfect harmony. To mirror Ikus, I needed to broaden my awareness, sharpen my abilities, and hone my responses. When Ikus slowed, I slowed. And when he sped up, I too sped up (at least to the best of my meager, two-legged means).

He paid attention to me when I walked when he walked, stopped when he stopped, ran if he ran, turned left when he did, paused in the middle, or faced a different direction. And there was so much more to mirroring than just repeating his position or direction or speed. A big part of the process was learning to mirror the energy Ikus was exerting and changing it to my speed. I needed to make sure I kept my energy in calm control and gave him a role model to emulate. It was not all physical; I believed Ikus had insight into my emotional body; my energy alone could affect the outcome of the day's lesson. Ikus could read subtle, unconscious details I was not yet aware of myself; like Shaman, Ikus scanned me with his intense stare. I tried to scan him back in an inquisitive way, to match his stare would be too intense, and could even appear predatory to the horse.

It would become a bigger challenge to not only mirror Ikus's body language, but to go beyond and grab the horse's thoughts and attention and change his energy level using my intent and body language. My heart was filled with hope for any animal I dealt with in the future. I was so excited about what had happened with Ikus that I would take as many opportunities to mirror feral, stubborn, scared, wild-minded canines and horses as I possibly could. I loved learning and honing this wonderful new art form. I was remembering, with this incredible horse as my teacher. I learned that with time and patience, I could change many hours of hard work into a simple dance of cooperation.

In the end, Ikus learned together that calm energy was better; we breathed deeply and connected as one in truth and trust. Ikus and I developed the relationship I had dreamed of, but it was short-lived.

I knew when I got Ikus that he would not be with me for long. He was nearing twenty years old, and shortly after our mirror bonding, I learned that part of his resistance could have been coming from a tumor that was growing behind his right eye. His loss of sight could have caused him to distrust me at first. I do not believe the mirroring caused him undue stress or made his cancer get worse faster. I discovered a photo that had been taken before our work together, and it was clear the cancer had started before I had gotten him. I was just so glad to have had the short amount of time I did have with him, and I will never forget the blessings he left me. Ikus passed away after two major surgeries to remove several cancerous tumors in his head. RIP, precious Ikus.

Tracy and Ikus. Photograph courtesy Kent Weber, 1999.

CHAPTER 18

Sister Wolves

Using what I had learned from Ikus, backed by the confidence I gained handling the two-thousand-pound horse and combined with intuition about animal behavior, I believed I could change the course of my personal wolf handling.

Around midsummer in 2002, a woman called on behalf of a friend who had two young wolves in desperate need of homes. Because of the urgency needed to pick up the pups, Kent and I immediately loaded our gear into a small Subaru and began the hours-long drive across the state of Colorado. We met up with the owner of the wolf pups in the parking lot of a large grocery store. Kent rolled down his window, and we chatted a few minutes; he seemed like a gentle, sincere man who had fallen on hard times, financially and personally. He had recently moved to Colorado, and he had previously been keeping big cats (lions) along with other exotic animals including the parents of the pups. The pups were growing too fast, and he could not build an enclosure to hold them as adults.

At that time, the pups were being kept at his remote mountain property, several miles out of town. We followed him to the property and agreed to retrieve the pups. We were a little concerned that we would find dog cross pups, not wolves. But we had committed to help and did not want to back out, no matter what we found. The man told us he had already placed the siblings of the pups and their parents. "These two pups were the last to go," he said right before we pulled out of the parking lot. I could tell he was sad that he had to find homes for all his animals.

We followed his truck into the mountain up a well-maintained, winding dirt road. My mind wandered to the homes and camping trailers we passed. After what seemed like twenty miles, he finally turned off onto an undeveloped dirt road. I looked around the property and saw lots of tall pine trees. We continued to follow him into what appeared to be vacant property, hidden behind a thick stand of trees. My eyes searched for signs of pups but found nothing. We drove around a large circle of trees, and anxiety began to come up in my chest as we pulled in; I could not immediately see the animals and felt uncomfortable.

I could not imagine where the pups were being kept, and there was no sign of an enclosure anywhere. We passed the only structure, a small camping trailer tucked in a grouping of trees; still no sign of wolf pups. We drove around the corner and just beyond the camper on the opposite side of the road, and a small gap opened up between the trees. There, we could see a fence poking out between the trees. That must be where the man kept the pups. I gasped in surprise when we got into full view. I looked at Kent in disbelief, saying under my breath, "Oh my gosh; that's the pup's pen?"

My heart jumped up to my throat, not in fear of them, but rather in fear for them. The man had gotten out of the truck and walked to the pen. I could see two pairs of furry little black paws stretched up, reaching the top of the four-foot livestock panel holding them. Up and down their paws bounced. It looked like they could jump out if they wanted to. As I watched the pups continue to jump up on the fence, I understood the urgency to get them out.

One steel livestock panel, measuring four feet by eight feet, stood nailed in between trees growing close together. It looked like the same size fence panel lined the back, keeping the pups enclosed, but they were quickly outgrowing their temporary holding pen. From the passenger seat of the car, I could immediately see the little black feet pop up over the top of the fence, again eager to greet the man.

The pups jumped up and down on their back legs for several moments. They were so excited to see the man; their little faces stretched up toward him. They desperately tried to poke their heads over the top of the wire to reach the man. Their little tongues licked at the air as they bounced, just like a pup begging food from an adult wolf. I could see the pups loved the man, and he seemed to care very much for them. I was astounded that the pups had not gotten loose before, or perhaps they had. Both Kent and I recognized right away that we were looking at wolves, not crosses.

Two shiny, striking black faces with bright, flashy yellow eyes looked up at us. The man was very sad the pups had to leave, but he hoped the sisters could become Ambassador wolf teachers one day. We agreed it would be wonderful if the pups were outgoing enough to be comfortable in public. We only stayed a few moments longer, as we had a long drive home. We loaded the two sisters into the car, I laughed because they suddenly seemed a lot bigger than they had when they were jumping around in the pen. At only four months old, they were growing daily.

"Oh, by the way," the man said as we finished loading the car, "I came up early this morning and fed the pups lots of raw chicken so they would be full for the ride."

I looked at Kent; we both knew what that meant. We were in for a long and stinky ride home. As we started back down the road, I turned around and looked at the two wide-eyed sisters huddled against the seat, pressed tightly together. They looked confused and scared. I talked softly to them and reached out my hand, but they just looked at me and did not move.

By the time we reached the end of the dirt road and turned onto the highway, one of the pups threw up the first round of chicken. Immediately, the foulest, most putrid smell hit the air. It took me back years to a time we were traveling with Shaman after a beaver trapper brought several whole beaver carcasses out for us to feed to the wolves. Although the thought of a wolf eating a beaver was unusual, it was not entirely impossible. We did not know if they would even eat the beavers, so we fed it out as a test. The wolf van was scheduled to leave the next day to do programs. We did not think anything of feeding a beaver to Shaman's pack, not realizing that Shaman would be an eager beaver himself, grabbing up the whole beaver and running off with it, protecting it from the others like it was his last meal.

By the end of the evening, Shaman had consumed the entire beaver. The next morning, the beaver feeding was pretty much forgotten about. We loaded Shaman and Lakoda in the van. The two canines acted sluggishly during the load. They slowly made their way up into the part of the van they would ride. We had a couple of volunteers helping on the trip. The two young women climbed in right behind Shaman and Lakoda, and down the road we went. As we reached the corner and turned down the driveway, Shaman's stomach suddenly turned, and he emptied the contents right on the floor, next to the unsuspecting ladies.

Panic hit. One of the girls shouted, "Stop! Let me out!"

The rancid, musky stench from the beaver was unbearable; it nearly brought out the contents of everyone else's stomach as well. Kent slammed on the brakes, and everyone piled out of the van in a hurry. He did the best he could to clean out the smelly beaver chunks, but it was an impossible task. The stench of dead animal lingered the entire trip and lasted beyond, creating an unpleasant atmosphere in the van for weeks.

Kent pulled the car over at the next exit. I reached around with a towel in my hand and proceeded to mop the mess off the seat and floor. The sisters continued to cower in the back of the Subaru. The pup with more white in her fur was drooling and her ears had dropped down to the sides of her head; she was the one that had gotten sick. Her sister looked peaked, too. The sisters were endearing little creatures with such innocence behind their golden amber eyes.

The young black wolves braced themselves, their eyes opened wide and pupils enlarged as we cruised down the highway at fifty-five miles per hour. Within a half hour of leaving their former residence, a four-hour puke-a-thon began. The smell was horrid but nothing like the smell of Shaman's beaver in the old Chevy van. After making several unplanned stops to clean up puke piles, we finally arrived home. The pups had certainly puked up all the chicken and would be ready to eat once they got over feeling carsick. I hoped that new surroundings and people, along with other canines, would be enough distractions to take their minds off leaving the kind man who had raised them and the long car ride. The pups were shy but slowly began to warm up to us soon after their arrival.

The little wolf sisters were friendly and curious enough; they had a real chance of being Ambassador wolves one day, maybe even joining Rami to begin their work educating the public. One sister was primarily black, and the volunteers decided to call her Raven, after the original founding wolf. The other sister had a black back, but her belly was white. We decided to call that sister Magpie, after the black-and-white bird from the same *Corvidae* family as the raven.

It was clear the two sisters first needed to learn how to be comfortable in the human world. We spent the remaining summer socializing the pups to visitors at the sanctuary, and they learned to greet newcomers. At six months old, Raven and Magpie followed Rami's lead in the Ambassador wolf program. At the time, Rami was nine years old and had matured into an outgoing people wolf. She brazenly paraded around in front of audiences of hundreds of people at a time. However, Rami hadn't always been as confident; her self-assurance developed when she grew into her role as a teacher.

Although Rami developed the ability to appear docile and comfortable inside a classroom, she remained a wolf in spirit and behavior. She somehow seemed more subdued in public. But when it came time to teach the insecure little feral spirits, unsure of the human world, to be brave in public, especially outside the sanctuary, Rami's presence was often not enough. She could only set an example, and if the pups followed her example, then great. If not, it would be up to me to figure out how to keep the sisters calm. And that was a big job. And there were some quirky aspects in Rami's behavior that I did not want the pups to pick up.

Rami, a very high-strung wolf with an abundance of energy, always commanded attention. Not in the way of being petted like a dog, rather in the way of direction or leadership. During exercise walks, Rami insisted on putting herself in front, taking the lead, whether she was ready to or not. Like the scout of a traveling party, she would get out in front, and then she would lose her nerve and often become confused as to where to go. She grew stressed that she was in the lead. Rami would also belligerently pull on the lead. She became headstrong during walks and often pulled her handler around. And that was challenging for me.

After all the time I had spent being dragged behind the big boys, with more than thirty sprained ankles, broken fingers, sore shoulders, and other injuries, I did not look forward to being pulled around by a little seventy-pound wolf. Sila had given me a new understanding of how I could connect with an animal on the lead, but Rami would not listen like Sila did. When Magpie and Raven arrived, Rami was a senior and set in her ways. I did try to work with Rami, the way I had learned to work with from Ikus or Sila, but she was resistant. It seemed true: You can't teach an old dog, new tricks. But Rami set a good example for the pups in other ways, like getting in and out of the bus and being brave enough to walk on a leash in a new environment. I felt it was up to me to change the energy and the way we worked with the sisters instead of working to change Rami, who was set in her ways.

I thought it best to let sleeping dogs lie; after all, Rami amazed me at how well she adopted the sisters as her little pack, and she did her best, managing them in her own wolf way, and that was good enough. My plan was similar to when I first got the idea to mirror Ikus. During the beginning of my horse work, I was already formulating how I would adapt the horse lessons to the wolves. I planned to experiment with the wolves using horse-training techniques, and if it did not work out, I would stop. I would not do anything that might lead to undue stress on the wolf or abuse them in any way; that was first and always foremost.

As for the natural horsemanship exercises I was learning, I thought the wolves might understand and respond as horses did. Why not? I questioned my thoughts and reasoned that if humans, wolves, and horses all had similar behavioral patterns in response to life events (fight, flight, or freeze), then it may absolutely work. This could lead to a much more natural and easier way to connect with the wolves. Becoming aware of this was like being given permission from the creator to go ahead and practice what I thought were the appropriate horse exercises on the wolves. Then the doors blew open, and ideas begin to pour into my mind. Promptings that I believed were coming in from a source beyond my humble knowledge or experience. I began to put together all the information I gained from my previous wolf experience and what I had learned from my first horses.

I had gained tremendous confidence handling the two-thousand-pound equines. Combined with my instinct and intuition about animal behavior, I genuinely believed I could change the course of my Ambassador wolf handling simply by changing my approach to the wolves. I had spent more than a decade handling wolves in old, repetitive ways, and I knew the wolves needed variety just as much as I needed to change things for the better. I was so eager to learn. I decided to leave the door open for evolution, no matter where the source of my inspiration came from.

Rami, an awesome Ambassador wolf, selflessly educated countless thousands of people, ten times over, about her wild kin. As a representative of her species, she was perfect, at least in her world. For me, the little wolf had some behaviors I wished would change. I considered Rami's conditioning part of the past generation of learning how to handle wolves in public. That generation of wolves was raised to believe they were more dominant over people, due to the way we rewarded the wrong behaviors without realizing the consequences. I wanted to evolve my work with subtle leadership and even more intuition; to me, intuition is the key to everything in my life, and I believe I will carry that with me after I die. The old saying "You can't take it with you when you die" is wrong, at least when it comes to building our spirit or character.

I believe I will take my instincts, intuition, and more with me when I go; that's my plan, anyway. I also believed that changing the ways I physically handled the wolves by becoming more conscience of my actions could do nothing but help in the long run. I already had the natural ability to bring a wolf into a room, and with a positive outcome. What more could I expect if I brought a new kind of consciousness to my animal handling?

I had gotten a small taste of what it felt like to walk in a true connection with Sila, and I wanted more. I longed to constantly be in connection with my animal friends, in ease and confidence. And I wanted to walk all future animals in that way, not just experience a few blessed moments of connection here and there. During that time, I recognized the power my rope lead could have on the relationship I had with the animal. Like a divining rod of communication, that rope would teach me where I could find cooperation and where I would find resistance or fight. In the same way a horse could be in pain from a bit, a canine could experience discomfort or injury from improper leading.

Over time, walking Sila improved because she made an effort to work with me too. Rami, on the other hand, wanted her way all the time; like a spoiled princess, she tended to pull me around. Whether I was walking a wolf on a rope or riding a horse with a bit in its mouth, I tried to perfect a form of art. For me, this was an intriguing art form, and I wanted to know more; most importantly, I wanted to handle a rope or bit well. I was thirsty to craft my art and practiced walking in unison with the wolves every chance I got. I spent years free walking with horses, often mirroring them daily.

With Rami in the bus as a role model for the young sisters, for the most part, we were off on a smooth start. I say "for the most part" because we had not stopped for exercise yet. As the bus rolled down the road, the rattling noises coming from inside the old custom built Marine Corps eagle bus kept the pups alert. Rami loved to explore and was a scout at heart; she was excited, too, and watched out the window to see where we were going. The newly recruited travelers spent their time seeking safety in the familiarity of sibling bonds. They huddled under Rami's kennel deck, tucked up against one another, cautiously looking out at every noise. The first exercise stop would be in a large cement parking lot in Kansas. We leashed up the canines and prepared to get off the bus for a short break to stretch our legs.

I learned from many different horse trainers how to lunge a horse, which was good exercise and also developed respect in the animal. This exercise could even be used to overcome a horse's fear, circling the horse around an object or place of fear until it came to terms with the fear on its own. This exercise taught me to direct the horse's energy and power in a forward movement. Controlling a thousand-pound horse was impossible under some traditional terms, but I learned to direct the animal, which was different. *What a great way to approach the wolves too,* I thought when I heard this. I remembered that no matter how hard I tried to control Shaman while running, he usually got the best of me.

On many occasions, I tried to circle the wolves around me; it felt natural, but I never made the connection that I could direct the wolves in a fashion similar to horse training. Lunging horses for respect and exercise was a standard practice for many. In fact, learning to lunge horses opened my mind farther to the potential that wolves might respond in a similar way to the horses. And anything I learned about horses after that, in my mind, I applied to the wolves too. I assumed that intentionally circling the wolves around me would keep their attention on me, and that might be a way for me to help them overcome their fear's too.

As a new little experiment, I created an invisible circle around my body, about three feet in diameter. And while the wolves were on leash and the leash was in my hand, they could circle around my body at any time we were moving, as long as they remained within that three-foot diameter, and the leash had slack. I thought that if this worked, I might resolve the intense pulling and, therefore, walk more peacefully.

Once the wolf became excited, got distracted, and left my invisible three-foot perimeter, the animal would get a nudge of gentle but firm pressure on its neck through the collar. Unless of course a rabbit ran out in front of us, then pressure became an eye for an eye. I would need to bring more strength in through my handhold and in turn put more pressure on the collar. I then would hold pressure until the wolf corrected itself and came back into the space. Once they returned to my invisible circle, they would be rewarded by an immediate release as the leash went slack.

When the canines were ready to get off the bus on their first outing, Kent walked out ahead of everyone with Rami. Raven followed close behind. I was tethered to Magpie, who rushed eagerly to get off the bus behind the others and than spooked at the door. But a bigger problem began once Magpie hit the parking lot pavement; she immediately stopped short in her tracks and looked around. Raven and Rami were well on their way across the lot and did not even look back, and Magpie began to panic. She immediately jumped back into the bus and ran for the safety of her kennel. Memories flooded my mind of times I had been in this situation with previous wolves running for safety.

I recognized I had rewarded the wolves for being fearful without meaning to. I held tight to Magpie's lead; I could feel explosive energy come into my hand as she tensed up, realizing that Rami and her sister had left her behind. Panicked Magpie bolted past and jerked me back out the door. Again I found myself standing on the black pavement. This time, Magpie paused a moment longer, and her attention went to a man walking in the distance. Her head went up, and her eyes widened. Once Magpie caught sight of this person, she went to the next level of fear.

I braced my body and wondered what she saw when she looked at the guy. He was far enough away to not pose any threat to her. Maybe she was scared for Raven, because she and Rami were close to where this man was walking. The others were now too far ahead of Magpie to reassure her. I was on my own. The bolt and jerk dance was in my immediate future, and I tried to go with it. Not knowing the exact direction I would be going in this dance between human and wolf made me feel anxious.

As Magpie darted up and down the bus stairs, I worked to stay calm and get her attention back on me and her feet back out on the pavement. I did my best not to step back on the bus, because I wanted to give Magpie the impression that we needed to move forward outside and not backward into her kennel. It would have been easier if I just put her back in the kennel and let her sit out the run. I could sit down on the bench, relax, and watch the others from the window. But then this text would have never come to be.

I will always remember the frantic movement of Magpie's legs, sprawled out, toes digging as best they could into the pavement, her little tail tucked up under her belly. A heightened sense of fear reflected back to me from her eyes, locked wide open. I felt compassion for her, but I knew that if I jumped back on the bus, my behavior would reinforce her fear, and then she would be set up to spend the entire trip in fear. It looked as if she was heading that way already, whether it was because a man was walking across the parking lot or because she was reacting to something horrible she believed was about to happen. She wanted to practice the flight behavior. I did not want to accept a fearful outcome for her. I wanted her to get over her fears and be a content, happy wolf.

I waited, my boots firmly grounded to the cement, a good strong grasp on her as she panicked all over the entry of the bus. The next time Magpie's paws landed on the ground, I used my intent and physical power to direct her to run a circle around my body, instead of letting her jerk back and forth. I had to keep a firm hold on her, and after a moment, I got her to make one complete circle around my body. Once she learned she could run around behind me that seemed to help. But back into the bus she went. Her force and drive to get away remained high. I had to remind myself to keep grounding my boots again and again before she knocked me off my feet. She was pulling me that strongly.

Rami and Raven were up ahead, exploring; I could see them out of my peripheral vision, and they did not even seem to notice Magpie was missing. They sniffed the pavement curiously as they trotted along in the direction of the strange man.

Holding on to Magpie that day took me back to an experience I had with a Thoroughbred horse a year earlier. The first time I had the horse in halter out in the field behind the barn, she freaked. I remember standing at the end of the rope attached to this horse as she proceeded to throw a temper tantrum. I was asking her to face something she was afraid of, and she wanted to flee. That was an eye-opening experience, because horses could potentially cause more damage than wolves.

If I could get through that horse experience, I reasoned, I could manage a six-month-old scared Magpie. For some reason, I had to muster all the courage I could that day and really ground my roots deep and thick through the pavement and into the earth below. Magpie pulled me forward, and in a maneuver I was well accustomed to, she turned abruptly back in the opposite direction. At that moment, her strength and intensity matched any horse. I had to work for a few moments at being patient and strong-willed to get to the point where I could direct her instead of reacting to her. Once she got to the end of the lead, and I successfully directed her to circle around me the second time, she seemed to begin to understand what I was trying to do.

Again she darted and pulled hard, lurching forward; her claws grasped the pavement as if I were leading her to a sacrificial altar. Again I worked to direct her energy around my body; panic began to well up inside of me too, and I suspected that circling the wolf was not going to work. Without knowing exactly what to do to help Magpie, I just stayed put, feet to the ground. We did circles again and again, until finally, she paused for a few seconds just to catch sight of the other wolves. In that brief pause, I realized that she was desensitizing herself to the man walking in the distance; she was now standing and looking at him instead of bolting.

It made sense to me that by allowing Magpie to run away, even for a brief second, gave her a small release, and when she was turned back around in the direction of the man and faced him (even for a split-second), each time she became braver. After a few minutes of circling and facing the walking man and then fleeing from him, Magpie began to relax a little. Although we were far from having a complete resolve of her fear, we had a plan of action that gave me tremendous confidence that we could get through this. With her sister Raven and Rami up ahead, Magpie chose to run in circles, but at least we were now getting away from the bus and moving forward. In that instant I recognized I could lunge a wolf like I had lunged horses!

As we neared the walking man, I could feel Magpie tense up again, and around in another circle she went. I circled her behind me so she could move away from her fear and release her nervous energy, and when I faced her back toward the object of her fear, she relaxed. After five minutes or more had passed with us spinning in circles, she began to realize she would be okay, and her circles began to slow down. Soon we walked right up toward the man, who by now had seen her coming toward him. I was glad I had spent so much time circling the horses. Working with the big draft horses, especially when they were scared or being stubborn, gave me the confidence I only recognized I had that day with Magpie. For a moment I enjoyed a newly found confidence I had never felt before in my prior work with the wolves.

Lunging Magpie in the same way I had done with horses was only the first step in modifying horse training for wolves. There would be plenty of opportunities to mirror the shy sisters, too. We had been invited to exercise the wolves in a tennis court, a secure and fenced-in facility where the wolves could safely be off leash to get some much-needed free time. The first time I tried to catch Magpie, it was a huge challenge, and she resisted being leashed. Kent and the others I worked with did not understand the level of connection I was hoping to make with the wolf sisters. And anytime I tried to explain what I believed, I was met with resistance. It was not that Kent did not believe I could do it, he just did not understand what it meant.

Mirroring wolves and horses became so subtle and natural for me that the people surrounding me often had no idea I was doing anything at all. What caused the most conflict for me wanting to move forward with mirroring was Kent. He was resistant to change from his old patterns of how to catch the wolves. All in all, this would be the ultimate test for me to make a stand for a new way to work with the wolves. After we turned the wolves out in the tennis court, we all hung around and played and laughed. Once it was time to get going, it was easy to catch Rami; she had no need to run away, as to her, the leash meant off to the next adventure.

When Magpie and Raven saw us coming with the lead rope in hand, however, they wanted to run away, especially when Kent went into play-bow (hunched over wagging his butt as if he had a tail) body language to catch the sisters. Anytime I would get near Magpie to catch her, Kent would do a play bow, and she would be off, running around in circles again.

I finally had to tell Kent, "Hey, let me try this!"

He looked at me like I was mad and yelling at him or something.

I told him, "She is reading your body language, and any time you play bow, she does the same; we are not teaching her to catch doing play behavior, we are encouraging her to run away from us. I am trying to present my body language as neutral and ask her to stop."

I needed to work one-on-one with her, to walk upright, hands at my sides, and move with the intent to be leashed. It was not easy that first time, but I did have success. More to my relief, Kent caught what I was trying to do and saw how quickly Magpie responded to my body language. After that, it was just a matter of time, and as it had with the horses, mirroring the wolves worked in the same way, with the same results. The remarkable part about working with Magpie was not mirroring her and getting better than expected results it was after a period of time doing so that the roles reversed and one day I realized Magpie was mirroring me.

Raven, Tracy, and Magpie. Photograph courtesy Kent Weber.

CHAPTER 19

Wolf Intuition

Magpie, a remarkably intuitive creature, seems to have the ability to see pictures we formulate in our mind's eye.

Being intuitive is as natural as using one's arms and legs as tools. I believe it is part of everyone (at least to those who deem it important and use it). Intuition and empathy go hand and hand; the easiest way I have learned to describe my own intuition is through empathy. I learned a profound and simple lesson about intuition from Linda Kohanov, an author and clinician and one of my teachers. I attended one of her classes and learned how to do a body scan. Linda asked everyone to assess their own individual body, to go through from the tip of your toes to top of your head, anywhere that you may be feeling pain, tension, or discomfort, and then to do the same on an emotional level and make a note of how you were feeling. After she described the lesson, we then split up and picked a horse to walk up to. Once I had an understanding of how I felt physically and emotionally, and I entered into the space of the horse, any feelings of discomfort that came up I learned belonged to the horse, not to me. How simple it was to learn this; I wished everyone would learn about empathy in school. Oh, how different the world would be.

Years later, after Rami had completed her service as an Ambassador wolf and Raven had retired to sanctuary life, Magpie traveled alone. Kent and I have experienced intuition from the wolves more times than we can count and on more occasions than we were aware of, until the following story happened, which especially made me open my eyes and pay more attention to the intuition of the wolf. Magpie was a remarkably intuitive creature; she has the ability to see pictures we formulated in our mind's eye. I know this because on my own, I conducted many spur-of-the-moment tests with the wolf, picturing in my mind different things Magpie enjoys, such as treats, and being astounded by how she responded. These little experiments, however, were not as remarkable as one very touching experience that happened on October 31, 2006, when we were visiting a good friend in the Catskill Mountains. Her family lives in an incredible house built on the side of a secluded mountain, and we enjoyed many visits with these warm and wonderful people.

They had invited us to a yummy Italian dinner and called to ask if it would be okay that an elderly woman, whom she recently met via a phone conversation, could join us after dinner to meet Magpie. At eighty-eight years old, Freda believed she was on her deathbed. When she learned a wolf would be visiting near her, she became very excited. One of her last requests was to meet a wolf in person. Freda had recently discovered that the wolf was her totem animal. She was wheelchair bound, on oxygen, and would require the aid of a special doctor to visit. When the car showed up in the driveway, a surprisingly very lively but weak old woman appeared. The doctor helped Freda into the house and sat her down on the couch.

I was reluctant to bring Magpie into the amazing house, because I was worried about the wolf's indoor etiquette. She had not been inside a house for a long time, and in case we had an accident, I wanted to be ready to prevent it if I could. But after we started talking with Freda, I completely forgot my concerns. She told us of her lifelong love of wolves. She had a special encounter as she was getting close to death, and a pack of spirit wolves had begun to escort her everywhere. She believed meeting Magpie would help her pass over, and she very much looked forward to getting out of pain.

We listened in awe to this incredible woman talk openly about her feelings and the life she had lived.

I told her how much I appreciated that she was speaking straight from her heart, without editing what she said to please others. She had that like-it-or-not attitude about her, and the words she spoke felt true. Freda's response was that at her age, all she could do was speak her truth. I envied the day I could do that, as I often found myself speaking to please others or saying nothing at all. When we brought Magpie inside the house, the wolf seemed to reflect the love she was feeling from Freda. This frail woman even sat down on the floor to meet her, and that was not easy. And when Magpie greeted her face-to-face, Freda nearly fell over. Magpie does have that effect on people.

Freda thanked us and our hosts for helping her achieve her dying wish and a lifetime dream. Later, Freda called our hosts and requested some of Magpie's fur as an addition to her medicine bag, a treasure she planned to wear to the grave. The final missing element was the wolf, and a tuft of fur would complete her bag. Early the next morning, a very clear intuitive prompting occurred with Magpie; what she did that morning still makes the hair stand up on my arms.

I had just gotten out of the shower and was getting prepared to walk back outside when our host came and asked me if I could get a little tuft of Magpie's fur for Freda. I replied I would try to collect some. It was October, cold enough that the wolves had grown in their thick winter coats. I ran a brush through her clean fur, and no hair came out. Magpie became annoyed at me and tried to move away from my hand reaching out at her, holding the brush. I put the brush down and grabbed a pair of scissors from Kent's medicine bag. I had hoped to quickly cut a small tuft off her back or shoulder without her being aware.

Magpie would have none of it. She began pacing faster circles around me, and I could not reach out with the scissors in case I accidentally jabbed her. I tried to explain to Magpie what the small piece of fur I needed was for and what it meant to this lady. I said how special it would be if Magpie would just stand still for a second and allow me to clip off a small tuft. She ignored me and quickly spun around me again, as if she were scolding me and telling me she would much rather get out for a run than get her fur clipped. Kent and I were rushing to get the wolf bus together, as we were behind in our schedule and had to leave early that morning. After a few rushed moments, I gave up, disappointed, and walked back to the house to tell our host to ask the sanctuary to send a tuft of fur to Freda, because I was having no luck retrieving any fur from Magpie.

I walked passed Kent, as he was getting ready to start the bus engine. He had the charging cord in his hand and was rolling it up, packing away the last of our gear. I made one final round of the house to make sure I had picked up the last of my gear before walking out. The next thing I knew, Kent came out of the bus with a big smile on his face, holding a tuft of fur in his hand. He waved it at me to see as he went by, pleased with himself. I was amazed and wondered how he got Magpie to hold still long enough. I had just been in the bus, and she was completely uncooperative for me.

Kent told the amazing story: he said as he got back onto the bus, Magpie was in the very back, getting into his bathroom bag, the same bag I had just retrieved. Kent walked toward Magpie into the wolf kennel, and when she saw him coming, she bolted out of the back room, carrying something in her mouth. He thought she had his toothpaste or shampoo, something smelly that she found to roll in. When he went in to retrieve whatever she had taken, he was shocked to see her turn toward him with a pair of scissors in her mouth. Kent was a little shaken at the irony of this; Magpie had never gotten into his bathroom bag and brought out the scissors before. It was as if she had heard our request for a small piece of her fur, after all.

I genuinely believe Magpie understood how important the piece of her fur would be for Freda and decided she better get it now. Kent said that Magpie stood completely still while he clipped a small tuft from her thick coat. I stood there with my mouth open, wondering how this could be; was this simply a coincidence? Magpie would have to dig in the medicine bag I had put back up high on the shelf, not easily reached from the floor. She had to work to get the scissors back out of the bag. How connected was this wolf to her human companions? Far more than I was aware of, truly a creature that inspired me on so many levels. Three months later, I heard from our friends that Freda peacefully passed away, and I could not help but wonder if her spirit pack was there to greet her.

CHAPTER 20

Seeing Shadows

Sally would surprise me by how well she used her intuition with the animals.

One summer day, a horse trailer arrived at the holding barn at the bottom of the sanctuary hill. Inside the trailer stood an old Thoroughbred mare and a very nervous appaloosa gelding. The mare was skin and bones; at thirty years old, she was in very poor condition. Standing behind her, in surprisingly good shape, was the appaloosa. At the time, a young woman had traveled all the way from the UK to spend a year at MW as a volunteer. Sally had no idea what she would be getting into when she arrived. She immediately fell in love with the horses, and since the appaloosa seemed in good shape, he might be around for a while and would need care.

Sally was excited to take on the care of the old horses for as long as they were comfortable, and she even named them. The appaloosa she called Brayson, and the Thoroughbred she called Cookie. We learned that Brayson's eyesight was diminishing, and it was quite apparent when you looked into his eyes. A cloudy milk film was covering them, and his eyes were dull and foggy; they did not look healthy. At eighteen years old, Brayson's body and mind seemed fully intact and healthy. I believe that when a horse like Brayson is with us for a short term, they have a purpose or a lesson to teach us.

Lessons we need to learn in life do not always present themselves the way we expect them to.

Brayson first met his traveling companion, Cookie, on the trailer ride. He immediately found security close to her. Once the horses were off the trailer, Brayson did not stray far away from Cookie's side. Brayson lost his home because his eyesight condition was progressing rapidly. The reason he had to leave was his changing behavior toward the other horses. Brayson was becoming very insecure and defensive. He would aggressively strike out at the other horses; this caused lots of stress.

We had seen this type of eye disease before in a couple of other appaloosa horses; someone suggested it could be moon blindness. Someone else said that Brayson's eye color was once blue; the first day I looked into his eyes, I could see the cloudy fog growing. His right eye was much worse than his left. I had been focusing on teaching others about mirroring that summer and had been talking to anyone who would listen, whether they wanted to hear what I had to say or not. For the most part, I received enough genuine interest to keep me going. I desperately wanted others to understand that simple body language could make a huge impact on feral, scared, or otherwise troubled canines or horses. Sally was a great candidate to practice with. She had a natural sense of the ideas I was talking about and was already doing many things for herself, such as using her intuition and being creative. She also had a strong confidence about her that the animals responded to very positively.

I believe that any human with the desire and intent to connect, in loving and positive ways, with troubled canines or horses was born with the tools to do so already within them. Anyone with enough self-awareness to think about how animals are seeing human body language, anyone carrying an open heart and following their intuition and instincts will understand these ideas. This is our ancient language, calling to us to remember all that we have learned in lifetimes before, and carried with us up to this exact moment in the universe of infinite possibilities.

We immediately understood the problems that Brayson's previous home was having with him and why he had been brought here. Once he was turned loose around the barn, he became a nightmare. Watching him run around was frightening. He did not know his boundaries and would frequently run into things inside the enclosure, including the fence. Clearly he was a danger to others and especially to himself. This alarmed everyone, especially Sally, and after watching for a couple of days, she became very stressed and sad for the big old horse. This went on for several days to the point where the entire staff had watched Brayson run into the fence and even a couple places into the barn. He had received several minor cuts on his legs and was clearly afraid of his strange new environment. He had yet to develop a relationship with anyone and did not trust new people coming around him.

Brayson stayed close to Cookie for protection, but he would move away if anyone approached. When Cookie stood inside of the barn, sometimes Brayson could not find her, and he would panic and run off, screaming. Brayson became especially fearful when the wolf howls echoed down the aspen valley, and that is when he did the most damage to the fence and to himself. Brayson was not interested in making friends with the people at all, including Sally. We could see that although his eyes were in bad shape and seemed to be growing worse every day, he was not completely blind.

Sally wanted to do whatever she could to genuinely help Brayson and Cookie, even in their twilight years, when riding was out of the question. After a few days of watching Brayson injure himself on things, Sally wanted to know if there was anything more that could be done to help calm him. My curiosity, of course, went to mirroring; I wondered if he could see well enough to communicate through body language. Cookie was in poor health, and soon she would be gone. Her death might potentially leave Brayson by himself. Other horses may come, but it was hard to know when that would be.

We could not guarantee an immediate companion for Brayson after Cookie. Therefore, we hoped he would make some human friends. My concern about mirroring him was that he might not see well enough to read physical signals, or he would become so freaked out that he would overreact and run through the fence. We had never worked with a horse losing his sight before, but I felt it was worth a try. With a little coaching, Sally began working with Brayson using mirroring and approach retreat (stepping into his space and retreating from it when he gave a positive response). When possible, the use of food treats helped, as long as they were given at the right time.

I could see that Sally had a natural confidence in her own abilities around the animals and a drive to follow through. I stood back and let her work on her own for a couple of weeks with Brayson, helping whenever I was asked.

When I visited the barn to see how Brayson was doing, I learned how he was improving and how the damage to his body had lessened. This was occurring simply by Sally using her intuition and body language, which gave me tremendous hope and excitement. I decided that what was happening between Brayson and Sally was too good to miss, and I would try to catch what I could on video. From that point on, I decided to record the coaching and make an inspirational visual lesson on the power of mirroring. Sally noticed that after working with Brayson for a while, he seemed to be able to see shadows and movements and still responded as if he had sight. The first day I started to film Sally and Brayson together, it was very clear that he was very genuinely afraid of people and noises around the barn.

That was understandable, because up the hill was the home of many wolf packs, and all kinds of noises would come down the small valley and land at the horse barn. I investigated what it would take to fix his eyes and contacted a few people who could help if a vet trip was in line. What I learned was discouraging. Yes, there was a potential surgery that could help him, but for how long was unclear. And when I told these people how old Brayson was, I got a resounding "No" for an answer. Perhaps if he were younger and had a life ahead of him, that might be different. With no funding to pay the vet for Brayson, we decided to do the best we could and simply make him as comfortable as possible for as long as possible.

For the time being, one of the first things we needed to do to was help Brayson become settled in his new surroundings. He needed help to quiet down and relax. Working with people like Sally, who were open minded to their own abilities and not resistant to being coached, helped make my job easier. More importantly, I felt so rewarded whenever I saw someone become more aware of his or her natural connection to animals. And I love to share this with people. I encourage anyone with a good sense of their own natural intuition to follow that as their guide in their work with animals.

I learned early on that intuition was the most important tool in my awareness of animals. Sally would surprise me how well she used her intuition with the horses. She also took a lot of time with Brayson and cared about him a lot. She worked with him little by little to make him comfortable. The first day I brought the camcorder into the pasture to begin to film, I had no idea what was about to unfold in front of the lens. I had planned to help coach Sally to be successful with Brayson as I filmed.

I gave her a little help about just where to put her body and when to move, and what energy level to use to get Brayson to respond faster. Then I was distracted by something interesting. I noticed Brayson react to Sally coming near him. He avoided her approach and took off, running blindly across the pasture. That was not the interesting part. It was how he ran that concerned me. I began to think he had another kind of disease, something we did not know about yet.

The more I watched Brayson, the more it seemed to make sense as to how he was using his legs; he was doing it for survival. Because of his diminishing eyesight, he was throwing his legs farther forward to help him "see" where he was going. Outward, like antennas, his hooves would go, farther forward than I thought was normal. In spite of this, it was easy and natural for Sally to keep her body language gentle and calm and keep her intent clear to Brayson. It was very pleasing to see how well he read Sally, despite his eye problem. Our intent was to be able to walk out to the barn to catch Brayson and help him live a calm existence in the time he had left.

It was clear that Sally had grown very fond of Brayson in the two weeks she had been working with him. At first, he wanted little to do with her, but she did not take that personally and kept working. This touched my heart. While I was filming, I watched Sally move with Brayson as he took off across the pasture and ran right smack into the wire fence. Oh no, I thought as I quickly turned the camera off. I begin to wonder whether this was such a good idea after all.

"He used to run into the fence much harder than that," Sally said in a reassuring tone.

I reluctantly turned the camera back on, not knowing what would happen next; I certainly did not want to see any fence injuries.

The two continued on; human and horse moved around the field in unison. It was not an easy or a perfect unison, yet as Sally worked to replicate the exact movements and energy of Brayson, he was getting it; he seemed to understand. He would trot off, and so would Sally. He would stop, and Sally worked to stop as close to the same time as Brayson. And if he turned in toward her, she would stop and take a step backwards to give him a reward. Brayson seemed to look for an opportunity to get by Sally and then take off again; Sally would fall back behind him, trying to keep her body alongside of him. It was a huge challenge, since obviously he was a much faster animal. I watched and could see when Brayson would hook into Sally, the very moment the two truly connected.

When Sally mirrored Brayson, he would stop and ponder what all was going on, and in a good way. You could almost see a switch go off in his mind and a huge weight lifted off his shoulders. This was something I could not see when I worked with Ikus. All her previous work in the days before was about to pay off big for both Brayson and for Sally. I could see the role of the mirror reverse, and Brayson mirrored Sally at times. He was beginning to slow down to her movements. Each time, Sally would relax more and offer Brayson a calmer and calmer energy.

Any time Brayson tried to move away from Sally, she learned to anticipate which direction he was going to go. She would then move that way too. That gesture alone would catch Brayson off-guard and make him stop to contemplate what she was up to. She would stop, too, and relax, even take a deep breath and let it out in a noisy fashion. He would relax too. The physical work involved for Sally to do this in the right way was incredibly time consuming. The exercise part of mirroring is not for the weak of heart or anyone looking for a quick fix.

Mirroring can take a long time, especially at first, and Sally was looking to permanently resolve Brayson's fear. Every day for nearly two weeks prior to me getting the camera out, Sally would work to calm Brayson and put a halter on him. She would practice mirroring Brayson, anywhere from a few minutes to around an hour, just a little time every day, in good weather and in bad weather. Using her body as her main communication tool in a pressure-then-release way, she soon began to flow with the rhythm of the horse. The more I watched Brayson, the more I admired him. I noticed what super keen senses he seemed to have, in spite of losing his eyesight.

At all times, Brayson knew exactly where Sally was. His body signals said so. It probably took Sally longer to calm Brayson than it would have taken a horse with full eyesight. And Brayson may have responded to her body language communication a little slower, but for him, it was just the right amount. One of the things I loved about using body language to communicate with Ikus was it became second nature. The more I worked to refine my own grace and movement with the horse, the more it became like a dance or union of togetherness; from then on, my relationship with Ikus was true and trusting. For me, this kind of work with horses felt right and true to my heart, like an art form, if you will. And nothing meant more to me than to see another person achieve the same connection with a horse.

After many hours of work in front of the camera, Brayson finally stopped long enough to investigate the halter. Sally did not try to put it on his head immediately; she simply moved it around, reminding him about the sounds it made and letting him smell it. It was a cold and gray day; the snow was beginning to fall, and Sally wore a heavy jacket, snow pants, and heavy winter boots. It was not an easy task to move with a horse on the ground, restricted with that much bulk. Sally then did something unexpected. She had been giving Brayson horse treats in his food, and she intuitively realized that she could make noises with her jacket and teach Brayson to come to her for a reward. That might help the process of gentling him and allow him to trust her more quickly.

I thought this was clever and watched as she got him to quiet down using her body language, and then she got his curiosity up by urging him to come in close with a scratching noise she made, running her hand up and down the front of her nylon jacket. At first he was worried, but then she managed to get a cookie into his mouth at the perfect time. This made him inquisitive. The next time she scratched her hand up and down to make the noise, he was not as nervous about it. Brayson explored the noise and got a cookie reward. Sally did this repeatedly until he very clearly understood that when she made the noise, he could come right up close to get a cookie. He was a bit unrefined about how he grabbed the cookie; Sally said at one point he really reached out and aggressively grabbed it, pinching her finger hard.

He probably had not visited with a dentist for a tooth float in some time. Likely his teeth had some sharp points, which made getting pinched by him even more painful. I was in awe of Brayson, who was standing quietly and relaxed near Sally; this was the exciting part. I was over the moon with happiness at the success Sally had achieved with Brayson. At that moment, Brayson seemed to be saying he needed a friend to help him trust again. Sally achieved a level of trust and connection by reflecting Brayson's own movements and energy back to him. To Brayson, Sally looked like a genuine candidate, coming from her heart without force, ropes, or some other scary thing a senior horse losing his eyes would be fearful of.

We assumed that Brayson had all the basic halter training he needed as a younger horse and that he had previously been ridden. Even though we were not seeing any result of this at the time, in fact, what we faced was quite the contrary. On that first day of filming, we decided to not put the halter on him, even though Sally felt she could do so. He was doing so well and relaxed with her, we thought that might be what he needed. Shorter lessons that ended on a huge positive note, such as this one, always created a better energy in the horse for the next time. Sally did one more short exercise.

Like a dancer, Sally gently moved with Brayson up a small incline hill, where he quickly (within moments) settled down. He stopped and paused, waiting for the next move. Sally then coaxed him up to her with the noise of the nylon vest, rewarding him with a cookie. What tickled me at the end of the session was standing in front of the barn, watching Sally prepare to feed the horses for the afternoon. All this time we were working in the field with Brayson, Cookie was waiting (not so patiently) inside the barn, neighing to Brayson through the wooden and metal barn walls. Cookie had been shut in the barn to keep her out of the interaction between Sally and Brayson.

Sally walked away from Brayson into the barn to let Cookie out and bring hay and cereal out. Brayson knew exactly what was up and came rushing over to the front of the barn. In his big hurry, I felt that he did not see me standing near the entrance, so I spoke up out loud to him. Once he heard my voice, he stopped in his tracks. Wild-eyed, he stood looking at me; back and forth his head turned as each eye examined the unfamiliar voice standing in front of his food place. I could tell that he did not see me at first. Like a deer caught in the headlights, he glared in my direction.

I stood still and talked to Sally in hopes Brayson would become comfortable with my presence and relax. Brayson, still hooked into Sally, turned his head back toward the entrance, anticipating feeding time. He was so relaxed and content. This was the most relaxed I had seen him the entire time he had been at Mission: Wolf. *What a relief,* I thought to myself, *to see Brayson doing so much better, thanks to Sally's care and love.* As Brayson waited for his food, he began to yawn. Sally let Cookie out of the barn; she stopped at the entrance and began to eat hay.

Brayson yawned again. He kept yawning as he waited. He dropped his head down and yawned yet again. He turned his head sideways and let out deep guttural sighs of relief. There was so much yawning going on that writing this made me yawn, even as I remember this, and I can still feel the wave of sleepiness that came over me at that moment. Brayson's face gestured with a slight shake of his head. This motion was followed by a big release of nasal fluid that sprayed out in front of him.

I smiled. I was standing far enough away that I missed getting sprayed on. As I stood there and observed Brayson, it was as if I could see him change right in front of my eyes. He seemed to be releasing pent-up anxiety, perhaps from many years of built-up fear. What a great experience for Brayson to find a friend who truly cared enough to go the distance with and for him. He could now spend the rest of the time he had left content and loved. Sally walked out of the barn, carrying a bucket of senior feed for Brayson.

As she walked away from the barn to feed him, I watched Brayson turn and follow her. Sally set the large five-gallon bucket, containing a few cups of grain, down for him to eat. He had become so in tune with the nylon rubbing noise that Sally's jacket made that his head turned automatically as she squeaked past. He continued to follow Sally's movement as she walked back toward the barn to get more hay. As he turned back toward the barn, Brayson completely lost track of where his food bucket was placed; in that instant, I could see just how poor his eyesight was. He searched side to side for his lost bucket, which was positioned right under his feet. Sally returned with a large armload of hay, shaking it out onto the ground. She asked me if I thought he was coming along well.

I answered, "Yes, he is amazing, very much so, especially compared to Cookie."

"I see him like one of your horses now," Sally said, with hope in her voice.

"He could have a future," I said, also hopeful for Brayson's longevity.

She replied, "I'm glad you think so."

I left the barn for the day and decided to return to film the next day. When I woke the next morning, I was so inspired by what I had seen the previous day, I could not wait to get back over to the barn to film Sally and Brayson again. I was filled with so much anticipation for the outcome: the catch! Immediately upon starting, I noticed how much more relaxed Brayson was when Sally approached him.

This was so exciting; the hard part seemed over. Sally was able to walk right up to a once-terrified appaloosa horse with the halter in her hand, prepared to catch him. With little hesitation on Brayson's part, Sally moved in toward him, and he did not move away. She reached out toward his nose, in hopes he would be curious enough to touch the halter and smell it. When he did, Sally gave him a reward.

Cookie, stood outside with Brayson that day. The old mare appeared fully in tune with the gentle mirroring Sally was doing with Brayson, even though it was not directed at her. To my amazement, I watched as Cookie hooked in and mirrored Sally and Brayson. Horses are such incredible creatures. Sally moved right up next to Brayson; she easily reached her arms up and gently slid the rope around his neck. That was it. Brayson remembered the halter, and when he began to pull away, Sally held pressure; once he released, so did she. In just a few minutes of work that day, I could see Brayson's body language completely shift, and I believed he would now live out the remainder of his life in peace.

Brayson had gained tremendous trust for Sally. His whole appearance had changed; he now looked at the girl with appreciation, trust, and curiosity. Not fear. Within a moment, Sally had the halter on Brayson. That day was nearly anticlimactic, because it took so little time and effort on Sally's part to halter Brayson. All her hard physical work, calmness, persuasive energy, and time had paid off tremendously for Brayson. After the work she did with Brayson, using clear intent, mimicry using body language, and her own intuition, followed by a little cookie reward after he had a breakthrough, Sally had bonded with the horse. Brayson had made a friend with loving, comforting energy during his final time, significantly reducing his fear and its result: running into and getting caught up in the fence.

Sadly, Cookie was put down shortly after this experience. Her old body was no longer absorbing nutrition from her food, and she was wasting away. Brayson spent the rest of his days as a different animal, in a good way. He became recognized as a great teacher and was loved by Sally along with several others. He lived beyond this bonding time, up until his eye condition worsened. Within months, the disease covered his entire right eye.

We could see how irritating this was for Brayson, because he spent a lot of time rubbing his eyes. When Brayson began to feel pain and discomfort; the only humane thing left to do was to help him start the journey across the rainbow bridge. To cross the dimensions and leave behind the pain, and going blind behind, to run free and meet up with loved ones in greener pastures. That would be the best possible outcome for Brayson. Thanks to the inspiring work of Sally, we had already done what we could by teaching Brayson to trust people again and give him love. Cheers to a great teacher, thanks Brayson for inspiring me to continue this work.

CHAPTER 21

Tracing Nature

To truly understand an animal, we must first strip away all preconceived judgments and notions about what we think we know or have learned or been programmed to believe about that animal. The animal's behavior is a direct reflection of what we deeply believe about ourselves.

In all the years I have spent studying, developing, and practicing my art of mirroring wolves and horses, a question frequently appeared in my mind: "Could I mirror a wild wolf or horse?" I do not believe in going into the wild to mirror animals that are surviving on their own (quite frankly, they need as much space away from ever encroaching humans as they can possibly get). But experience has taught me there are enough feral and wild animals in captive or domestic situations to satisfy a lifetime of curiosity about cross-species mirroring.

The following summer, I had the opportunity to work with feral wolf pups. Eight stunning four-month-old wolf pups had made their way, via a large horse trailer, to Mission: Wolf, their new home. I was excited but a little nervous too; this was the first time we had taken in this many animals at once, and that would prove to be challenging and bittersweet. It was a mixed group of pups; four were Arctic wolf pups, and the other four were gray wolf pups. Kent was vacationing in Alaska at the time, fishing for salmon. Although he knew the pups were coming, he was not able to return when they arrived. Without Kent's influence and help, we were as prepared for the arrival of these little creatures as we could be. I watched eagerly as the horse trailer carrying the pups slowly pulled up the steep driveway hill and turned around, backing down into the parking lot.

I could hardly wait to see the little wolves; my heart welled up with emotion and tears came into my eyes as the truck came to a stop. I walked out to greet a very generous man who drove many hours to pick up the pups and bring them safely back to Colorado. I was practically out of body with emotion by the time we stepped in the trailer to see them. Bringing in puppies was a very welcomed affair. Their arrival felt like a long overdue boost of happiness and inspiration; the sanctuary wolves would be overjoyed too. Too many years had past by caring for elder horses, wolves, and wolf dog crosses and being there as they grew old, got sick, and died.

I became attached to each and every one of these animals; every time one passed away, it was devastating to me. Wolves, the "fierce" predators, had a side to them that not many people understood or were willing to witness. And the lucky few who did know the true nature of wolves rarely acknowledged their gentle, brilliant sides. The animals were so easy to love and cherish; they were family members or dear friends, soul mates, if you will, or an extension of my own heart. I felt uncertain about what I expected my first impression of the pups to be. But when I got an eye full, they took my breath away. They were stunning, incredible.

I was sure by the terrified look in their eyes that they did not feel the same about me. Scared and pushed as far up against the back of the horse trailer as they could get, they seemed to shake at the uncertainty of what was to become of them. I looked around and saw the wild little things had done quite a bit of damage to the trailer's interior during the ride: the seal between the doors was stripped out with their teeth, they pulled up the flooring, and they tore down parts of the walls. They would be glad to get out and have some fresh air, sunshine, and space to run. And the man, I was sure, would be glad to get his trailer back before any more destruction occurred.

A rainbow of young wolves lined the back end of the trailer, looking up at us and wondering about their next move. This was one of the most exciting times in the sanctuary's history. How blessed we were to have these incredible creatures come to us. I moved to the back with the pups to help the man load each one into a kennel. I hurriedly took hold of the furry scruff of the top of the first pup's neck, and the little animal went limp in my hand. Lifting it toward the kennel, we guided the pups inside. I could feel a wave of terror shoot through me as I quickly and gently lifted the second pup up off the floor. It stayed motionless and did not react.

I was amazed at how heavy the pups were as I took hold of the larger black pup. As I picked him up, he looked up at me. I could see fight in his eyes but did not think much about it until it was clear the little wolf wanted nothing to do with being picked up. With an attitude and moves like a snake, the little pup reached around and took a bite out of my arm. Sharp little needle teeth went through the long sleeve of my shirt. My arm started to bleed, and soon blood soaked my shirt cuff. One by one, the pups were carried off to the Ambassador wolf enclosure.

We had hoped that by first introducing the pups to Magpie, her outgoing nature might rub off on them. The best-case scenario would be the puppies becoming socialized with the Ambassador wolves. Later on into summer, if meeting people by living with the brave wolves proved enough to bring them out of their shy shell, they would stay put. If not, the shy wolves could be moved into more secluded enclosures and live in peace, with little people influence.

I was growing excited to see the pups run loose inside the enclosure and found myself hurrying to release the others. Once the kennels were all brought inside, we turned the pups loose with the adults. Chaos ensued as the pent-up little bundles of wild ran across the new habitat in every direction; with so many of them, they were going everywhere. I cannot imagine what Magpie must have been thinking. She had just gotten over a pseudo pregnancy, and the timing was great. If there was a time in a wolf's life where the human saying, "Be careful what you ask for," applied, it was that moment for Magpie.

It had been a while since I had last been around wolf pups, so long that I forgot how fast they grow. With their huge dish ears, long legs, and big paws, they were endearing. Magpie took to the pups immediately and cared for them with great energy, enthusiasm, and zest. Life went along smoothly for the first week, until one of the pups came up sick, and the next day he died. We were devastated to learn parvovirus was spreading throughout the puppy pack. When all was said and done, after frantic vet runs and stressfully waiting for test results, three of the beautiful pups had died. What a blow.

In the end, it was the more dominant pups with strong-willed personalities that survived. The meek or weak perished within a week. This was a scenario similar to any event that might play out in the wild. Regardless, it was a truly depressing turn of events for me. I felt heartbroken, responsible. RIP to those three little lost souls. I missed them dearly that summer. Weeks passed after the parvovirus had come and taken its toll; the remaining pups did not want to have much to do with people. Who could blame them? I myself was moving around the sanctuary scared and truly depressed.

A heavy feeling of helplessness lingered in the air. It seemed natural that the wolves could sense the energy and chose to stay away. One of the little Arctic pups seemed to show a spark of hope. It was as if he was saying, "I am still here and alive!" The little male did not come up to me when I visited the pups, but he did not run away either. When Kent returned from Alaska, he named the little guy Illiamna, a name he had found in his travels. Illiamna's little white face was so endearing and sweet, I longed to touch him, but I knew from experience where that would lead.

Illiamna would stand and watch curiously from a distance; of course, he would not let anyone approach him either, but he was not all together against people being nearby. As the summer of bummer passed into fall, and the aspen leaves began to turn yellow, the time grew near to load Magpie and the pack into the bus for the East Coast Ambassador wolf tour; it was less than a month away. Illiamna remained with the Ambassador wolves, because his curiosity toward people continued. Kent and I talked about how stressed Magpie was going to be to have to leave behind her adopted pups to travel, even temporarily. But I believed that I could socialize Illiamna with mirroring; we could take him with us for his own experience and to help ease Magpie's separation anxiety.

I decided that I would first introduce the leash to Illiamna and his braver siblings. I brought the thick wolf leads inside the enclosure with me. I walked around the upper half of the enclosure, gently shaking the ropes out and dragging them behind me. Magpie and Abraham knew exactly what was happening and excitedly ran around, wagging their tails in anticipation. Abraham, an outgoing wolf dog rescue, had become a star in his own right with people, so much so he even earned a sheriff's badge to prove his magnificence.

This is the kind of canine Abe is: he walked around with me, wearing his collar and modeling to Illiamna. This really intrigued the pups; they eagerly ran up behind Abe as he made the rounds, occasionally getting his lead rope stuck in a tree trunk and needing rescuing from the happy, playful pups. I constantly supervised from a distance, far enough away so the pups were comfortable with my presence, but close enough to help Abe. The pups were so funny when they came running in behind Abraham, grabbed the leash, and started off down the hill with Abraham in tow, running across the little valley. Abraham was not as entertained as I was by this, but it showed the pups were now ready to be introduced to the leash.

It was two weeks before we were scheduled to leave for the fall tour, and our first stop was to be at CU in Boulder. This was my ultimate test. Could I use the mirroring body language with Illiamna as I had with the other timid animals I had worked with? Up until that point, I had never had any close contact with the reluctant Arctic wolf. He had no reason to trust me. If I were to get him on a leash, it would be a miracle, the icing on my cake of intuitive mirroring. We would see.

I would finally get an answer as to whether intuitive mirroring would work with a wild wolf (or the closest thing to one I could get). I was not trying to prove anything to anyone but myself (except maybe a little to Kent, too). After a couple of visits, the pups became acclimated to Abraham dragging the leash around behind him. I grabbed the lead in one hand and moved my body and the lead next to Illiamna. At first, he was stunned and ran a few feet ahead of me. The very rough terrain with a steep hill was not my ideal footing to work on. As the years passed by, my bones had grown tired and sore, and my stiff muscles called out for smooth, flat land to work on. But I guess if this was going to be my wild wolf experiment, the ground was suited the theme.

I paused momentarily until Illiamna took a step out. When he did, I did too. He stopped and looked at me in a way he never had before. He then ran off toward the back of the enclosure. Being careful not to chase him or run directly behind him, I took a few steps down and then gently jogged with him, working to keep my body next to his, no matter where he was in his enclosure, even at a distance. I worked for about an hour with Illiamna and spent a lot of time moving and walking gently. Every day, within the first few moments of mirroring Illiamna, he would stop, pause, and contemplate me.

With every session we ended, we were closer to each other than when we started. Like Ikus in timing, we worked every day for two weeks, and one day, just using my body, I could get him to stop, and then I stopped him up against the fence, by a tree, inside one of the shelters; he was really calming down. I would reach out and gently stroke his neck and then leave him. He became more and more outgoing and curious. The day before the program at CU, I needed Kent to help me get the chain collar around Illiamna's neck. We then walked him out close behind Magpie toward the bus. Having his neck touched seemed to be a huge deal for the big white adolescent.

He was very sensitive about it. Once the collar was on, he became more awkward; because he was just learning about all of this human stuff, there was no way I could use a soft nylon collar.

I decided that I was going to go back to a weight-appropriate steel chain as a training collar, for safety measure. If he panicked and bit at the leash, he would not be able to free himself. As we left the enclosure, Magpie and Abraham ran out like professionals; Illiamna, on the other hand, panicked at being tethered to a human. Even when we kept Magpie and Abraham close by for security, Illiamna flopped around like a fish out of water, all the way to the bus. Once on the bus, like it or not, he had to face Kent and me, up close and personal, on a constant basis. We did our best to ignore him the first few hours in the bus so he could make a safe place for himself. Ignoring Illiamna inside his kennel that first day helped to take pressure off and gave him personal space.

That next day, I quietly celebrated my success mirroring this feral young Arctic wolf as I walked him confidently in front of four hundred people at Colorado University in Boulder, where my whole wolf experience began more than twenty years prior. Illiamna played with toys, solicited dominance from Magpie and Abraham, and walked near the audience, closer than he ever had walked in front of visitors at the sanctuary.

Most importantly, Illiamna looked up at me with trust building in his eyes, and through his body language, I could see he was becoming more comfortable around people. That trip started out with a lot of tension and fear; Illiamna walked on a thirty-foot lead so he could have as much free space as he needed. And believe me, he spent most of that time at the end of that thirty feet. It would take the whole six-week trip to develop a baseline trust between the wolf and me. But when we returned to the sanctuary, Illiamna was walking at my side. I felt that I had accomplished my wild wolf mirroring experiment, and it went much better than I ever dreamed. Illiamna now had a new frame of reference about people. He graced public programs for the next two years, and after appearing in front of thousands of people, he retired to sanctuary life.

During that same time, I assumed that I would never have an opportunity to work with a true wild horse. And I honestly forgot about it until two years later, when out of the blue, I received an email from a woman who needed to find a home for a wild mustang gelding caught by the BLM that she had previously adopted. And although the horse had been worked with minimally, there had been some setbacks. This was a very challenging decision for the woman to make, as she loved the horse dearly and did the best she could, but the mustang had become fearful and unpredictable. This horse would be my chance to work with a wild caught mustang, one that had problems trusting people. And if this worked out, it would be the icing on my cake of mirroring wild-minded, feral, or fearful wolves and horses.

When the day came for the mustang to arrive, I watched the stock trailer back into the parking lot toward the holding paddock. I could see a striking black figure through the metal slots as the trailer got closer, and I could feel how nervous he was. His head was up and his eyes were wide as his nostrils flared in and out. Once the mustang was unloaded, I could see why his owners had concerns. When he stood in the holding paddock, he was braced to bolt in any direction if it came down to that. His eyes were wide open, and he paced back and forth, looking for a way out. Any time a person approached, he moved as quickly as he could to get away from them. I called him Merlin, in hopes that some kind of magic would float in and help me (or vice versa, help the horse).

In my opinion, Merlin was the most challenging and potentially dangerous test of mirroring I could find anywhere. Not only was he a wild animal, he did not trust people, and I was warned that he would strike if he felt threatened. For the first couple of days, I did not try to approach him. I let him have some time to adjust to his new surroundings and horse friends. After a few days, when I finally did decide to approach him, instead of walking straight up to him, I moved with him side by side. Because he was temporarily housed a small corral, I did not want my energy or my movement to become fast; by the way he acted, I believed such action could cause him to go over the top of the fence panels. So periodically during the day, when I would walk out to feed him or check on him, I would gently and quietly mirror his movements for a few minutes at a time.

When he would stop, I would stop in the same step and then walk away. After a week or more of Merlin acclimating, we had a muck workday. This included several people, wheelbarrows, rakes, lots of noises, and unpredictable movement all around him. I knew this would really terrify him and decided it would be a good idea to have everyone working with me that day mirror Merlin and introduce the tools to him. About ten people showed up to help, and they were all excited to meet the new horse. So the first thing we did before we started to work was carry the pitchforks and rakes out to Merlin's paddock. I was nervous about this, because I did not know what the outcome would be.

Most importantly, I did not want to overwhelm Merlin and cause him even more fear. Desensitizing him to the people and the tools would be enough. Wheelbarrows would take longer; he was already fearful when I was pushing one around by myself. Merlin looked at the wheelbarrow as it rolled low to the ground and made a hissing noise; he wanted to run away.

So we would wait another day (or month) to work on the wheelbarrow. I had no time line working with Merlin. He was older when he arrived, and I was older too. I wanted to take all the time necessary, for both our sakes, to do a peaceful and patient job gaining Merlin's trust.

Each individual person gently approached Merlin holding a rake in hand and moved slowly and gently with him. When he would stand and be quiet, the person would back out of his space. After each person mirrored Merlin for a moment or two, Merlin settled down and ate his hay. Needless to say, we had a successful workday, without causing the wild horse stress. This was exciting for me, because now there was an animal that I could teach others to mirror. Illiamna and Magpie would have had a lot of stress if I allowed others to mirror them. I felt tremendous excitement that Merlin would be a great teacher and help me get the message of mirroring out to the world. It turned out that all the magic I needed was right inside of me. It had been there all that time; I simply needed to remember it was there.

Several years later, in 2013, I got an urge to research intuitive mirroring on-line, in part for this book. Surfing the web, I found a Wikipedia definition for "mirror neuron," which surprised me. What had I been doing naturally all those years was explained; it was not a supernatural power. The website also explained the triggering that I felt and saw in the animals I mirrored within the first few moments, when their brains recognized what I was doing. As I close this book, so ends an era of mirroring wolves and horses to prove something to myself. As I get older and my joints stiffen, I find it more challenging just to walk. I no longer have the stamina and agility I once had as a long distance runner.

My dreams are now of an easier life, one of sharing with others my experiences and encouraging them where I can. But mostly I desire to return back to my artist's nature and simply be in joy with the animals of my life. To be natural with my horses and dogs and to know they trust and look at me with as much admiration as I have for them.

I have been blessed with much success using body language, intuition, and more to connect with animals. I felt it was my duty to write about my experiences so others can pick up where I left off and take animal communication to the next level. It is my sincerest wish that my stories inspire you as the many incredible animals have inspired me. Their lessons helped me change my life in ways I would have never believed possible had I had not experienced these lessons myself.

I have strong feelings that anyone open to this kind of work can mirror what I have done. However, I will not be held accountable for any form of animal abuse or cruelty resulting from misunderstanding my intent. My intent throughout my life has come from pure love, and I enjoy working with shy, feral and scared animals— not against them. I wrote this book to inspire new and natural ways to be with animals; I cannot take responsibility for anyone else's interpretation (or misinterpretation) of my words. For anyone wanting to mirror my footsteps, the responsibility for your own actions and results are up to you. I wish you the very best in true connections with the animals in your life!

Tracy Ane Brooks

Anyone interested in contributing to Mission: Wolf, please see the website www.missionwolf.org or mail directly to Mission: Wolf, P.O. Box 1211, WestCliffe, Colorado 81252.

ABOUT THE AUTHOR

Tracy has walked wolves into schools, universities, and museums like the Smithsonian Institute. She's brought them through challenging studio sets like those of The Today Show and Mr. Rogers' Neighborhood, and she has presented wolves to countless audiences across the US for over twenty years.

Tracy has been instrumental in building Mission: Wolf, a captive wolf sanctuary in Colorado. Her main focus is ensuring the wellbeing and contentment of the wolves. Tracy is one of those unique people who possess a deep understanding of instinctual connection to animals. After spending ten challenging years working hands-on with wolves, a horse came into her life.

Tracy embarked on a study of horse training, desiring to discover for herself the magic behind horse whispering. What she learned was to listen to the horse and mirror its natural behavior. Tracy wondered if she could use what she learned from horses on wolves. After all, predators and prey all have the same foundation of behavior: flight, fight, or freeze.

Tracy learned to mirror a horse named Ikus and resolved his run-away behavior in a simple, natural, non-evasive way. Ikus reminded her that these abilities to work with animals were within her all along. What followed was an intensive study of mimicry or mirroring wolves and horses. Many years of groundwork paid off when Tracy had an opportunity to mirror Illiamna, a feral wolf that she presented to over four hundred people at Colorado University in Boulder after only fourteen hours of moving with him. The icing on the mirroring cake was the opportunity to work with a troubled, wild-caught mustang.

A Walk in Connection is based on Tracy's life of learning to connect with animals. Her personal stories are intended to inspire, empower, and contribute to the greater global understanding of communication with other species.

CPSIA information can be obtained at www.ICGtesting.com
Printed in the USA
LVOW11s0607020115

421146LV00002B/4/P